Wood Knocks:
Journal of Sasquatch Research
VOLUME II

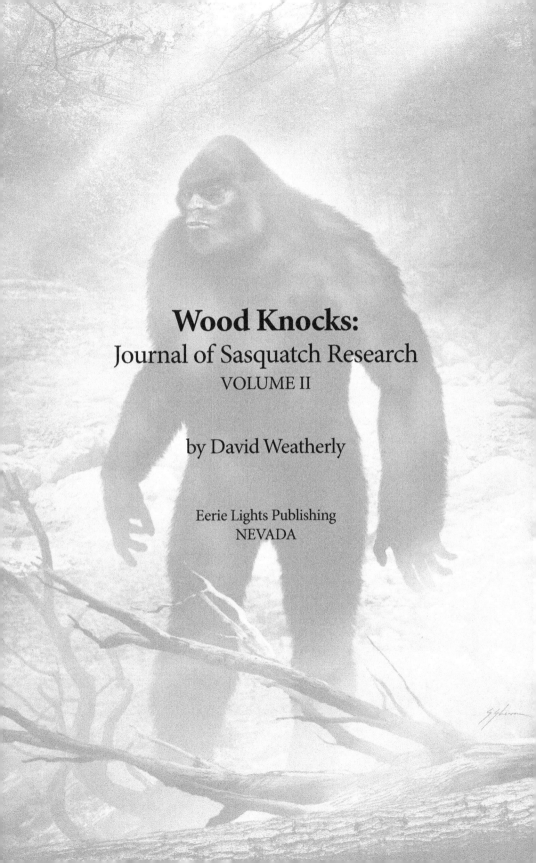

Wood Knocks:
Journal of Sasquatch Research
VOLUME II

by David Weatherly

Eerie Lights Publishing
NEVADA

Wood Knocks:
Journal of Sasquatch Research
VOLUME II
by David Weatherly

Copyright © 2017, David Weatherly and Eerie Lights Publishing
All rights reserved.

"Interdimensional Paraphysical Sasquatch," by Rosemary Ellen Guiley,
is copyright Visionary Living, Inc., 2017. Used with permission.

No part of this publication may be reproduced or transmitted
in any form or by any means, mechanical or electronic, including photocopying
and recording, or by any information storage and retrieval system, without permission in writing
from author or publisher (except by a reviewer, who may quote
brief passages and/or show brief video clips in review.)

ISBN: 978-1-945950-03-2 (Paperback)

Published by:

EERIE LIGHTS

Eerie Lights Publishing
Nevada

Cover by: Sam Shearon
www.mister-sam.com

Edited by: A. Dale Triplett
@DaleTriplett

Interior design by: SMAK
www.smakgraphics.com

Printed in the United States of America

Author's Introduction

Welcome to the second volume of Wood Knocks: the Journal of Sasquatch Research. If you enjoyed our initial outing, hold tight, because you're in for another round of fantastic pieces by some of the best minds in the field of Cryptozoology.

The stunning cover for this edition was created by artist extraordinaire Sam Shearon. His depiction of the legendary Patterson-Gimlin encounter of 1967 is a fitting tribute to the film that has intrigued people for fifty years.

Who better to take a look back at the iconic film than the director of the International Cryptozoology Museum himself, Loren Coleman? Loren has written a number of important volumes for the field and I'm happy to have him on board for this issue. His piece, "Fake News: How Wallace's Fake Footprints Fused With The Film," addresses an important aspect of the iconic film and contains tidbits that many are unaware of.

Christopher O'Brien weighs in with the first part of his exploration into Bigfoot reports from Colorado and Northern New Mexico. It's a region rich in encounters and likely deserves a full volume in and of itself. Chris has a long history of investigating the area and he's the perfect writer to address the sightings.

My own contribution this time around looks at the potential of Sasquatch in Nevada. There's much more to the Silver State than the lights of Sin City, and the mountains and vast wilderness could be home to something as yet unexplained. From Native American legends to modern sightings, there are ongoing stories of giant creatures in the wilds of Nevada.

On July 10, 2009, the first of what would turn out to be a wave of sightings was reported to members of the Pennsylvania Bigfoot Society. Long time cryptozoologist Eric Altman brings us a chronicle of these fascinating accounts in his piece, "The Chestnut Ridge Encounters." Multiple witnesses and numerous sightings make this an amazing story that still leaves investigators scratching their heads.

Tongue twisting title of the issue goes to Rosemary Ellen Guiley who presents us with "Interdimensional Paraphysical Sasquatch." Don't be intimated by the long words though, Guiley addresses a very controversial area of research: is there a connection between the creatures known as Sasquatch and reports of strange lights in the skies? Yes, we're talking about UFOs and before you shut down the idea, give the article a read and ponder the possibility that it may be something more researchers should examine.

Texan Jeff Stewart takes a look at, of all things, the Goat Man. Are stories of bipedal man-goats all hysteria and fiction, or is there something more to the encounters? Are these sightings, in reality, Sasquatch accounts? Stewart opens the door to several possibilities and raises some interesting questions. Mistaken identity or strange evolutionary sidetrack, his article will help you look at Goat Man accounts in a new light.

West Virginia boy Dave Spinks recounts tales of hairy beasts in the wild, wonderful state of his birth. From family encounters long untold, to recent sightings gathered during his investigations, Spinks opens our eyes to the fact that West Virginia is a hotbed of Sasquatch activity.

British cryptozoologist Richard Freeman is back again in this volume, presenting a paper on the Indian Yeti that Rudyard Kipling would be proud to read. Freeman has undertaken numerous expeditions to exotic locations around the world searching for mystery animals, and it's always a pleasure to read about his adventures.

Once again, the journal has been edited under the watchful eye of editor Dale Triplett who showed no mercy in crossing t's, dotting i's and checking facts. Although he does like to take his sweet time doing so. The gorgeous layout is courtesy of graphic arts guru Eddie Kaddi of SMAK Graphics — and his genius and creativity are a blessing to this effort.

So, sit back and enjoy as we delve back into the world of the elusive and mysterious creature known as Sasquatch.

- David Weatherly

Wood Knocks | Journal of Sasquatch Research, Volume II

Table of Contents

Fake News: How Wallace's Fake Footprints Fused With The Film — 1
by Loren Coleman

Bigfoot Reports from Central Southern Colorado/Northern New Mexico — 17
by Christopher O'Brien

In the Footsteps of the Indian Yeti — 43
by Richard Freeman

Interdimensional Paraphysical Sasquatch — 59
by Rosemary Ellen Guiley

Legendary Encounters with West Virginia Sasquatch — 77
by Dave Spinks

The Chestnut Ridge Encounters — 99
by Eric Altman

Texas Goat Man — 133
by Jeff Stewart

Silver State Sasquatch — 143
by David Weatherly

Contributor Biographies — 169

Fake News:
How Wallace's Fake Footprints Fused With The Film
by Loren Coleman

The year 2017 marks the 50th anniversary of the filming of a Bigfoot walking calmly along a sandbar of Bluff Creek, a tributary of the Klamath River, in the Six Rivers National Forest of northern California. The two filmmakers, Roger Patterson (February 14, 1933 – January 15, 1972) and Robert "Bob" Gimlin (born October 18, 1931,) recorded the alleged hairy hominoid October 20, 1967. Henceforth, the footage has been called the "Patterson-Gimlin Film" and the subject has been nicknamed "Patty."

Fifteen years ago, one of the most misunderstood debunking attacks against the Patterson-Gimlin footage occurred. The film was declared a hoax in some quarters and how it became an alternative reality for the media was remarkable. Indeed, the episode left most people in the general public with the impression the footage had been overturned and revealed to be a hoax.

It all began with the *real* news that Ray Wallace died. Who was Ray Wallace?

The first attention to Bigfoot in modern America began in Bluff Creek, when a road construction team in 1958 came across large hominid tracks. The tracks were first found and cast by Jerry Crew, one of the site's bulldozer drivers, hired by owner Ray Wallace and supervised by site foreman and Ray's brother, Wilbur.

Allegedly a trickster in the field, Wallace was ignored or disregarded for years as "a noted creator of questionable cinematic

Bigfootage." Wallace used to tell reporters he had seen UFOs 2000 times, Bigfoot hundreds of times, and since the early days, claimed to John Napier and others that he had film footage of Bigfoot a year before the Crew footprint finds in 1958. To the dismay of expedition supporter Tom Slick and Bigfoot hunter Peter Byrne, Wallace insisted in 1959 he had captured Bigfoot, but when Slick put down some money, Wallace failed to produce a Bigfoot. Wallace told critic Mark Chorvinsky that he was the one who told Roger Patterson where exactly to go on Bluff Creek that fateful day in 1967, when Patterson was to finally capture Bigfoot on film. Of course few Bigfoot researchers believed Wallace's claim. As Chorvinsky pointed out in his anti-Bigfoot articles, Ray Wallace said he had many films of Bigfoot, which he floated around as "new" pictures of Bigfoot to various researchers until someone would take the bait.

In December 2002, the media declared Bigfoot dead. How? Through the creation of new hoaxes. On December 10th, *Pittsburgh Post-Gazette* columnist Tony Norman wrote: "Sometimes it takes a deathbed confession to put a stake in the heart of long-cherished beliefs. When Ray L. Wallace died of heart failure at 84 last month, he took a sizable piece of American mythology with him."

No "near death" revelation really happened, but that didn't stop such a characterization from taking root in the minds of the media – and hence, the general public.

In fact Ray Wallace – a longtime Bigfoot "researcher" considered by many to have instigated hoaxes concerning the famed cryptid – had spun his stories for decades. Several misstatements of fact were published or broadcast repeatedly in subsequent years following the original reports of his death, manufacturing a 'hoax' mythos that had no basis in fact. For example, five years after Wallace's death in 2007, in an article published by the *San Francisco Chronicle* upon the death of Bigfoot researcher Archie Buckley, it was noted that Ray Wallace made a "deathbed" confession that his wife was in a gorilla suit for a Bigfoot film. The assumption was he was talking about the famed "Patterson-Gimlin film" of Bigfoot taken at Bluff Creek on October 20, 1967. This is a complete fabrication – but the misinformation continues to be published.

I have continuously placed on the record the full unfolding of how the newspapers, television, and magazines took the death story of a Bigfoot prankster and extended it to encompass the Patterson-Gimlin footage, a pivotal piece of evidence. We need to gain insights into the making of the modern myths now associated with this episode of media mania with a short review of some specific examples of the journalistic untruths presently associated with this story.

Ray Wallace died November 26, 2002, the day before Thanksgiving. After sharing an obituary I had written about Wallace with the *Seattle Times*, reporter Bob Young interviewed me via phone and email on December 3, 2002, and in the following days. On December 5, the *Seattle Times* published their article, which has become known as the "Wallace hoax" piece. A dramatic Dave Rubert photograph of a Wallace relative displaying fake wooden "Bigfoot" feet, said to have been used to "create" Bigfoot in 1958 accompanies Bob Young's "Lovable Trickster" article.

Longtime Canadian Sasquatch researcher John Green's reaction was swift. He said that what the Wallace relative is holding "certainly is not a mold for the 1958 Jerry Crew 16" 'Bigfoot' cast, of which I have a copy, but it definitely is either a mold for or a copy of a 15" footprint of the type found by Bob Titmus and Ed Patrick in a Bluff Creek sandbar later the same year, of which I also have copies…As to Ray Wallace having started the whole thing, however, Rene Dahinden and I in 1957 saw a tracing of a British Columbia footprint cast that was a much closer match for the Jerry Crew cast, and that cast had been made in 1941."

This is a significant point. Bigfoot did not pop onto the scene in 1958, although that is the year the name came into widespread use. The Native traditions of hundreds of years cannot be ignored, and the old reports and evidence (pre-1958) have been around for decades. Even before the coining of the word Sasquatch by Chehalis Indian agent J. W. Burns in the 1920s, from a Native Canadian set of names, knowledge of the hairy, upright, apelike giants of the woods was already in the record, especially from ethnographers. In cryptozoology Sasquatch was what we call "ethnoknown" to the Natives, whether in Canada or in the United States of America.

This reminds me of exactly what happened with Christian Spurling's 1991 Loch Ness Monster "revelation," which the media called a "deathbed confession" (even though it was given two years before he died in 1993.) Spurling said the 1934 "Surgeon's Photograph"

3

of one of the Loch Ness Monsters was only a toy submarine made with plastic wood (although that material didn't exist in 1934.) The British papers declared, "Nessie is dead." Debunkers forgot to talk about the second photograph and more. The cracks in the "deathbed confession" slowly began to show, thanks to investigative journalist Richard Smith of Princeton University and others. The 1934 "Surgeon's Photographs" were never that important, except as an icon anyway.

As to this Bigfoot hoax claim, never mind the original Jerry Crew casts do not match the Wallace fake feet. Never mind we all knew Wallace was a prankster. Never mind Wallace wasn't able to put one over on any of us in 44 years. Never mind that no one can actually show how the hoax would have been produced. The media was constructing a new world of Bigfoot myth making.

Bob Young's article set the scene for a flood of badly written items, flowing forth faster than the speed of your cable modem. The original *Seattle Times* article was hastily and harshly rewritten by wire services and electronic outlets, facts were minimized to make sensationalized copy, and the outcome has been a morphing of Ray Wallace's alleged 1958 hoaxes and family films into his being responsible for the 1967 Patterson-Gimlin footage (even though that was never said.)

How did the Wallace story spin out of control, to the point of fostering a worldwide belief of Wallace creating the whole Bigfoot phenomenon — including the Patterson-Gimlin film footage too? The specific evolution of this new media hoax can be seen clearly in how this leapt from one newspaper to the next.

Bob Young's *Seattle Times* article for December 5, 2002, has this segment: "[Mark] Chorvinsky believes the Wallace family's admission creates profound doubts about leading evidence of Bigfoot's existence: the so-called Patterson film, the grainy celluloid images of an erect apelike creature striding away from the movie camera of rodeo rider Roger Patterson in 1967. Mr. Wallace said he told Patterson where to go near Bluff Creek, Calif. to spot a Bigfoot, Chorvinsky said."

The article continued: "Ray Wallace dismissed the film as a hoax and said he knew who was in the suit. 'Ray told me that the Patterson film was a hoax, and he knew who was in the suit,' Chorvinsky said. 'Michael Wallace said his father called the Patterson film 'a fake' and said he had nothing to do with it. But he said his mother admitted she had been photographed in a Bigfoot suit'. 'He had several people he used in his movies,' Michael Wallace said."

As is typical of the USA's Associated Press, a rewrite was prepared, and on December 6, 2002, the AP wire version included this edited paragraph:

"[Ray] Wallace said he told Patterson where to spot a Bigfoot near Bluff Creek, California, Chorvinsky recalled. 'Ray told me that the Patterson film was a hoax, and he knew who was in the suit.' Michael Wallace said his father called the Patterson film 'a fake' but claimed he'd had nothing to do with it. But he said his mother admitted she had been photographed in a Bigfoot suit, and that his father 'had several people he used in his movies.'"

Next the story jumped the ocean, and an article, for example, published this misleading paragraph in Edinburgh's *Scotsman* on Saturday, December 7, 2002: "Mr. Wallace later persuaded his wife to dress up in a monkey suit for 'Bigfoot' photographs, and he told Roger Patterson, a rodeo rider, to set up his camera to film the famous footage, shot in 1967, which supposedly showed the creature walking up the hillside."

The above and more were misunderstood or misread, and rewritten as the following in the *Evening Telegram* of London later on that same Saturday, in an article headlined, "That's not Bigfoot, that's my wife," written by Oliver Poole, their correspondent "based in Los Angeles." Other news outlets such as Singapore's *Strait Times* picked up the story, apparently repeating this mistake.

Poole's article reads, in part: "Mr. Wallace continued with the prank for years, producing photographs of Bigfoot eating elk and frogs. These, it emerged yesterday, were, in fact, members of his family – usually his wife Elna – dressed in a hairy ape suit with giant feet stuck to the bottom. The most famous evidence for Bigfoot's existence, the so-called Patterson film, a grainy, cinefilm image of an erect apelike creature, was taken by Roger Patterson, a rodeo rider, in 1967. It was another of Mr. Wallace's fakes, the family said – he told Mr. Patterson where to go to spot the creature and knew who had been inside the suit."

The story then jumped back across the ocean, to land on Sunday, December 8, 2002, in Vancouver's *The Province*, in an article by Stuart Hunter entitled "'Fake' Sasquatch flick won't halt Bigfoot hunt": "Despite a stunning claim last week that the most compelling film footage of the apelike creature is a fake, Bigfoot hunters say they won't stop pursuing their elusive and smelly quarry. The family of Ray Wallace admitted after his recent death from heart failure in California that while the Bigfoot footprints were huge, the hoax was much, much bigger. That was no man dressed in a gorilla suit in the infamous Patterson-Gimlin grainy black and white film footage from 1967 – that was Wallace's wife Elna."

Reporter Hunter even then uses an earlier quote from the *Seattle Times* article that was only about the pranks with the fake footprints, not about the Patterson-Gimlin film, and places it as his next paragraph after the above: "'He did it for the joke and then he was afraid to tell anyone because they'd be so mad at him,' admitted Dale Lee Wallace, the hoaxster's nephew." This juxtaposition caused all kinds of problems.

Therein you have the makings of a media hoax. First it began with Bob Young's mostly factual item (although filled with claims from the Wallaces) about Ray Wallace's death, and how the family said he used fake feet, allegedly, in 1958, including opinions and remembered claims of hoaxing. Then it goes to wire service and column creations, and finally to the jump that "the Patterson film is a fake by Ray Wallace with his wife in the suit" – something no one in the Wallace family ever said.

Remember this is the only quote that matters:

"Michael Wallace said his father called the Patterson film 'a fake' and said he had nothing to do with it." – Bob Young, *Seattle Times*, December 5, 2002.

So what if Ray Wallace said he talked to Patterson and showed him his films? Of course Patterson would have listened to this spinner of tales. Roger Patterson was a Bigfoot hunter in the late 1960s, and as an amateur researcher, he went around and did research. That meant finding those that were there, in Bluff Creek, in 1958, and reinterviewing them. Such behavior makes total sense, and Patterson never hid any of what he was doing. Patterson talked about visiting and interviewing Wallace in his 1966 book. *Strange Magazine's* skeptical editor, the late Mark Chorvinsky, with great fanfare, makes it a cornerstone of some conspiracy theory about Wallace and Patterson. Wallace is, of course, going to say he told Patterson where to go. So what? Others have done the same, to give themselves greater importance in the history of

Bigfoot.

By January 2003, when the media writers decided to compose something about Bigfoot or the Wallace fiasco, they would often carry forth these "newly" created myths into their reports. On January 3, 2003, Inside Edition did a segment titled "Bigfoot Hoax," in which they framed – uncritically – the Wallace family's stories, and then claimed Ray Wallace created everything to do with Bigfoot, including linking the Patterson-Gimlin footage to his hoaxes. (My appearance on this program to give a balanced stance on the developing story was heavily edited and cut to a few seconds. Such production occurs in reality programming, but it was unfortunate that a broader view was disallowed in this sharp editing.)

This same day, in the otherwise rather balanced front page *New York Times* article, "Search for Bigfoot Outlives the Man Who Created Him," reporter Timothy Egan turned to discredited Bigfoot Central hobbyist Cliff Crook as his "authority" to proclaim the Patterson-Gimlin footage a "fake." Here the link between the 1958 alleged Wallace hoax is mashed together with unfounded opinions on the 1967 film.

On January 9, Scott Herriott's "Segment 7" report on CNN's NewsNight was broadcast. Herriott's field production presented a good beginning —though highly edited case— against the Wallace claim (despite the fact the Wallaces withdrew from Herriott's and John Green's request that they show how the 1958 prints were made.) However, it was host Aaron Brown's introduction and final statements (the "outro") that diminished the report. Brown made Herriott appear to be an obsessed eccentric for "still believing" in Bigfoot.

Fox-TV (then-owned by Rupert Murdoch) was next up on January 13, with a report on Shepherd Smith's Fox Reports. A teaser earlier in the show gives a hint of what was to be expected; it was a frame from the Patterson-Gimlin footage and the words "Trail's End" underneath. Shep Smith gives the introduction by bursting forth, Fox TV-style, by saying "Big Fake. Big Fat Stinking Hoax…"

Dan Springer out of Seattle does the reporting next. He begins with the clipping from the *Seattle Times*, saying the paper has pronounced the death of Bigfoot when it told of Wallace's passing. Wallace's son is shown talking of Ray, and then old photos of Ray – "who was a logger" in the PNW, are shown. The finding of tracks at a location by his crew moved the Indian lore of Sasquatch into Bigfoot. John Green (identified as a "Bigfoot Believer") is said to have done "five decades" of looking, and is introduced as one of those not convinced by the hoax. A short clip of Green shows him saying the "tracks are real." The reporter says Green gave him some fake feet to walk on the sand to try to debunk the "hoax." The word "tried" is used in the narration.

Reporter Springer then says the "timing" is "bad for believers" as "scientists" were "almost ready" to do some serious research, but now scientists are "ridiculing the famous Patterson film." (This is not true, as the January 9th broadcast on Discovery of Sasquatch: Legend Meets Science demonstrated by screening interviews of scientists who analyzed several facets of the Bigfoot question.)

Michael Wallace comes back on Fox-TV's report to roll his eyes and say he knows who was in the suit. Of course through editing in this "sound bite" Fox is using the Michael Wallace quote to make it appear as if he's talking about the Patterson-Gimlin film, when he really was discussing his mother in other films made by his father. The piece ends with comments about the "controversy" of Bigfoot being buried next to Wallace, with a camera pan of Wallace's gravesite.

Time for Kids, January 17, 2003, published an article full of errors. Called "Bigfoot? Big Hoax!" by Kathy Hoffman, it appears to have been rushed into publication. Beginning with the supposedly humorous line, "The real story: Dad was the ape-man!," the article downsized the Wallace claims for children. Using the phrase "recent confession" once again, as if Ray Wallace was hiding his prankish ways when he was alive, the use of the word hearkens back to the early "deathbed" confession media mistakes of December 2002.

Then Hoffman writes: "Most scientists agree that Bigfoot is nothing more than a very tall tale. Almost all of the footprints ever found have turned out to be manmade."

Of course, "most" scientists have said no such thing, and "almost all" of the footprints are not "manmade." Actually, studies by Dr. Grover Krantz, Dr. Jeff Meldrum, and trackers and forensic experts have shown exactly the opposite to be the case. Only a very small percentage of Sasquatch footprints are human-created fakes. Kathy Hoffman gets her statistics mixed up again when she says: "Jeff Meldrum of Idaho State University is one of the only scientists who believes Bigfoot could be real." More and more zoologists, anthropologists, and wildlife biologists are open-mindedly examining the evidence everyday, such as famed primatologist and anthropologist Dr. Jane Goodall.

The New Haven Register carried an article on January 21, 2003, by Abram Katz, entitled "Self-delusion casts a shadow on Bigfoot stories." After opening with the typical Wallace fake feet claims, and opinions on a "guy in an ape suit," Katz writes: "The question is – and this is a big one – if Sasquatch is an actual animal and has been seen all over the country, why has no zoologist, biologist, or hunter ever seen one?"

Of course, this is not a true statement. Many eyewitnesses have been "hunters," of course. The fact zoologists and biologists who have sighted Bigfoot in the past have not rushed forward has everything to do with the ridicule and academic discrediting that often awaits them. Despite that, zoologists and biologists *have* been Bigfoot observers. Wildlife biologists appear to be more frequent witnesses than is generally understood.

Throughout January 2003, we were treated to a hoax about a hoaxer's family, and then in the February 2003 issue of *Fate* magazine, Mark Chorvinsky – a skeptical magician turned magazine writer and editor, and one of the minor players quoted in Young's Wallace article – presented a column claiming Wallace was marginalized by "Bigfoot enthusiasts." Taking the research field to task for this "failure," he quickly assured readers Wallace's role "cannot be overstated." Actually, most of what Chorvinsky writes about in his column is so full of overstatements as to be a superb example of the genre.

First, let us take a look at his thinking and his logic. Everyone knew Ray Wallace was a hoaxer. What is most important in this article is for Chorvinsky (who died of cancer at the age of 51 in 2005) to establish he said Wallace was a hoaxer — before anyone else did. He sadly fails in this mission. Despite Chorvinsky's claims to the contrary, Wallace was mentioned in the literature from the beginning in 1958 as a prankster and a hoaxer. Even the Sheriff's Department in 1958 was questioning Ray Wallace about whether or not he was behind some of the tracks. When he uses an interview Bigfoot researcher Dennis Pilichis conducted with Ray Wallace, how does Chorvinsky ignore that the interview came well before Chorvinsky's own interest in the subject?

"Where did this information appear in their books and articles before I discussed it in 1993," Chorvinsky asks. Chorvinsky has decided to ignore what is in the literature. In 1989, I wrote a book entitled *Tom*

Slick and the Search for the Yeti. Talking of Slick's late 1950s and early 1960s Pacific Northwest Expedition, I wrote: "The expedition's cast of characters also included Ray Wallace and Ivan Marx, both of whom may have gotten into the hunt on the serious side of things, but from all accounts traveled down a dark path of greed and deception..." (I followed this with an entire exposé of Ray Wallace in 1995 in *The Anomalist*.)

Ivan Sanderson in his 1959-1961 articles, letters and a book noted the links between the road construction work, Ray Wallace, the people he hired, the first prints found and the sightings. Betty Allen told of the hoax investigations in her 1958 news articles. In the 1970s, Marian T. Place mentions the Wallace brothers and the early days of "strange happenings" around the track sites. In a 1988 book *Brave* that Chorvinsky seemed to be completely unaware of, early Bigfoot hunter Steve M. Matthes entitled his Bigfoot chapter "Big Hoax," because during his involvement with the Slick searchers in 1960, he came upon finds of fake tracks. These tracks clearly appear to match some of the Wallace fake feet. Even *Skeptical Inquirer* was there with pieces of the puzzle before Chorvinsky declared in 1982 the firm link between the Rant Mullens' foot fakes and Ray Wallace.

In his February 2003 *Fate* column, Chorvinsky tells the reader he was a ten-year correspondent with Wallace, as if this is special. He tells us Ray Wallace "admitted" to him to be using fake feet. This is no revelation: Wallace said that in letters to almost everyone. Wallace claimed to have seen 2000 UFOs, to know where a Bigfoot guarded a gold mine, and much more. And then there were the films. Lots and lots of films. Ray Wallace made some of the worst Bigfoot films in creation. They were so bad you could almost see the shoes the people in the store-bought gorilla suits were wearing. They fooled no one and took no one in – except perhaps the above-named columnist at *Fate*.

The late Mark Chorvinsky said the Bigfoot "believers" wish to "diminish the importance of such pivotal figures" as Ray Wallace. What is so silly about this is Ray Wallace was, yes, "diminished," as much as he was tolerated, enjoyed for his funny stories of Bigfoot coming out of UFOs, and yet nevertheless mentioned in the literature. Wallace was an admitted liar. Why is it as soon as he is dead the joke he is putting on all of us, instead, is to be taken as totally truthful history? Wallace is having a laugh from beyond the grave, and sadly, while he was alive,

Mark Chorvinsky was the medium channeling that séance.

Take for instance, Chorvinsky's attack on John Green, one of the most moral and sharing researchers in a field filled with sometimes feuding factions. Here's what Chorvinsky said about the man who happened to have been involved in Sasquatch research before the 1958 Bigfoot case even came into the picture: "Green, whose entry into the field was as a journalistic hoaxer ... knew that Wallace had no credibility whatsoever [but he] never once stated this in [any of Green's] books and articles. It was only after I [Mark Chorvinsky] began to write about Wallace and his innumerable fake films, photos, and tracks that suddenly Ray Wallace was discussed, and the only way that they could deal with him at this point was to act like he was a minor figure in the scheme of things."

John Green responded: "The reference to my entering the field as a journalistic hoaxer is about as near the truth as Chorvinsky is ever likely to get. I did write a story in an April Fool edition of my paper about a Sasquatch carrying off a tourist. That was two years before I encountered any evidence that the subject is serious. The remark is an attempt to mislead his readers of course, but no doubt he considers that clever. Since there was (and is) no evidence that Ray Wallace (or anyone else) could have faked the Bluff Creek tracks, and ample evidence that Wallace had 'no credibility whatsoever', what reason would there be for me to mention him in a book? If I write another book should I mention that Mark Chorvinsky has written nonsense on this subject and has no credibility whatsoever, or would it not be kinder just to ignore him for the same reason that I never mentioned Wallace, because he is irrelevant? And what possible reason is there for Mark Chorvinsky, knowing that Ray Wallace has no credibility whatsoever, to inflict on his readers false information that he got from Wallace? Specifically, why does he promote the nonsense that Ray Wallace told Roger Patterson where to go to get his movie, knowing that Wallace had also claimed to have taken 10,000 feet of movies of Bigfoot there."

Chorvinsky's February 2003 column thus became the ultimate example of how the media, even within the Fortean genre of *Fate* magazine, became an example of the media getting the Wallace story incredibly mangled in a tangle of personalities and personal views of the Bigfoot mystery – with no regard for the facts.

Newspapers and the electronic media have short-term memory

when it comes to hoaxes and the ability of the Sasquatch researchers to monitor their own field. Bigfoot chroniclers have noted fakery in their examinations of the history of Sasquatch evidence for years. Ivan Marx, Ray Pickens, Rant Mullens, and Ray Wallace are the individuals most frequently mentioned in the literature. However, every time a new prankster attempts to gain some publicity for himself, the media reaction is one of surprise and overall acceptance of the new tale as the "whole truth."

For example, in 1982 Rant Mullens said he was responsible for the 1924 Ape Canyon, Oregon reports, and the 1958 carvings of the feet that made the tracks at Bluff Creek, California. News reporters believed Mullens' outrageous allegations, much as the media is swallowing the Wallace family stories today. The Mullens' hoax admissions followed a similar trail as the Wallace fiasco, for it was used by establishment "skeptics" to make what Bigfoot author Mark Hall, in his book *Living Fossils* calls "loose and unsupportable statements" that all Bigfoot prints "could easily be fakes" (Daniel Cohen). Or according to Michael Dennett that "Rent Mullens" (his mistaken spelling) talked to one of the "hoaxers" of the Patterson-Gimlin film, and told Dennett the suit was made of bearskins. Hall demonstrates how Dennett's "skeptical" influence spread. Palaeontologist Leonard Krishtalka discusses in his book *Dinosaur Plots and Other Intrigues in Natural History* that the whole Bigfoot mystery is a ruse begun by "Rent Mullins" (further adding to the misspelling.) Other "skeptics" (like *Skeptical Inquirer* editor Ben Radford, before the Wallace melodrama) have used the Rant Mullens stories to dismiss a good portion of Bigfoot/Sasquatch evidence.

Why is the testimony of an admitted liar, the source behind quotes feted by a skeptical magician as the truth, and mistakenly conveyed by the newspapers to be believed at all? The media mixing of the lies and rumors with a few facts in the Wallace story is pushing this one to the edge. This is Ray Wallace's ultimate hoax and bitter seed.

Afterword

Several players in the Patterson-Gimlin footage drama have died. Future investigators are seeing the loss of the original Bigfoot hunters, searchers, and chroniclers of the 1967 event. Let me note some of those linked to the incidents at Bluff Creek.

Roger Patterson (February 14, 1933 – January 15, 1972.) Along with Bob Gimlin, held the camera to film the Bigfoot the two observed on October 20, 1967, at Bluff Creek, California.

Ivan T. Sanderson (January 30, 1911 – February 19, 1973.) The Scottish biologist and writer was the one who arranged the first showings of the footage to scientists, especially outside B.C.; Sanderson showed it seven times (1967-1968) to members and guests of scientific organizations in Washington, DC, New York City, Atlanta, and other locations.

Rant Mullens (February 10, 1897 – March 1986.) One of the original hoaxers linked to the Bluff Creek reports.

Bob Titmus (December 24, 1918 – November 15, 1997.) When Roger Patterson and Bob Gimlin claimed to have filmed a female Bigfoot at Bluff Creek in October, 1967, Bob came from Kitimat, British Columbia, to the first public showing in Vancouver, and then went on down to California where he allegedly made casts of eight tracks at the film site.

René Dahinden (August 22, 1930 - April 18, 2001.) The Canadian rights to the Patterson-Gimlin footage were purchased by Dahinden, and he was a major advocate of the footage.

Bernard Heuvelmans (October 10, 1916 – August 22, 2001.) Late in life the "Godfather of Cryptozoology" felt more critical than positive about the Patterson-Gimlin film.

Grover S. Krantz (November 5, 1931 – February 14, 2002.) Initially skeptical, Krantz later studied the Patterson–Gimlin film in full, and after taking notice of the creature's peculiar gait and purported anatomical features, such as flexing leg muscles, he changed his mind and became an advocate of its authenticity.

Raymond L. "Ray" Wallace (April 21, 1918 – November 26, 2002.) Wallace was a known Bigfoot track hoaxer. His death and his family's revealing of Bluff Creek fakery confused the media.

Mark Chorvinsky (March 4, 1954 – July 16, 2005.) Chorvinsky was an outspoken skeptic of the 1967 Roger Patterson-Bob Gimlin Bigfoot film footage, and quoted often by the media until his death.

Michael Dennett (June 20, 1949 – May 2, 2009.) A harsh critic of the Patterson-Gimlin footage, Dennett would often take his debunking personally within his remarks about Dr. Jeff Meldrum. His final published article "Science and Footprints" (*Skeptical Briefs*, September 2006) was about contradictions in accounts of the 1967 Patterson-Gimlin film.

John Green (February 12, 1927 – May 28, 2016.) The author of many books on Bigfoot, including *On the Track of the Sasquatch*, was one of the initial researchers to understand the footage's importance and secured a screening of the film before scientists at the University of British Columbia.

Mark A. Hall (June 14, 1946 – September 28, 2016.) Working first directly with Ivan T. Sanderson, Hall's later promotion of the gold standard of the Patterson-Gimlin footage crossed over its significance within the Fortean and cryptozoology fields.

The Author: Loren Coleman is the director of the International Cryptozoology Museum located in Portland, Maine, a 501(c)3 nonprofit founded in 2003. Among 40 plus cryptozoology books are:

Creatures of the Outer Edge (with Jerome Clark, 1978)

Bigfoot! The True Story of Apes in America (2003)

The Field Guide of Bigfoot and Other Mystery Primates (with Patrick Huyghe, 1999).

Fake News: How Wallace's Fake Footprints Fused With The Film

Bigfoot Reports from Central Southern Colorado/ Northern New Mexico

by Christopher O'Brien

Those keeping tabs on outbreaks of hairy hominid reports undoubtedly wonder as I do, why Colorado hasn't experienced more activity than it apparently has over the years. Sitting on the backbone of North America, the state features 53 mountain peaks with an altitude of 14,000 feet or higher, and this is the vast majority for the contiguous United States. The mountains in the southern Colorado Rockies and Sangre De Cristos feature seven peaks above 14,000 feet, and just over the border the highest mountains in New Mexico loom just to the east of Taos. Within these vast mountainous regions, there are countless millions of acres of remote wilderness with no roads, no infrastructure—plenty of room for a large population of Bigfoot to roam. Yet sighting reports are surprisingly only in the dozens. Why is this? Is this vast inaccessible region perfect Bigfoot habitat, or is it something else? Let's first look at what has been reported and then analyze our data:

Bigfoot Research Organization (BFRO)

When I began my research into Colorado Bigfoot reports, the first place I contacted was the Bigfoot Research Organization (BFRO). Many of the reports listed in the total database of encounters come from this hardworking investigative group and a big thanks goes out for all your hard work!

Much to my surprise, the BFRO database only lists 121 total

sighting reports for the entire state, with Park County at the state's center leading with 10. Adjoining counties Teller and Eagle to the north add an additional 15 to the band of reports that extends across the wilderness surrounding some of North America's highest mountains. These sighting report clusters occur mainly May through September, warm weather reports. Further east around the Pikes Peak region west of Colorado Springs and north into the Black Forest are clusters of October through April, cold weather sightings.

Another apparent main center of year-round Bigfoot activity is to the south into the southern San Juan and Sangre de Cristo Mountains surrounding the mysterious San Luis Valley (SLV). This concentrated area of activity also extends south into Northern New Mexico, with many sightings directly along the borders between Archuleta, Conejos and Costilla Counties in Colorado, and Taos Rio Arribas and San Juan County in New Mexico. This is the region I will be examining in this article. I relied on my own "mysterious valley" research as well as other several databases (including BFROs). I've attempted to collate as many independent reports together as possible, in an attempt to ascertain patterns or gain any other insight into Southern Colorado and Northern New Mexico's hairy hominid activity.

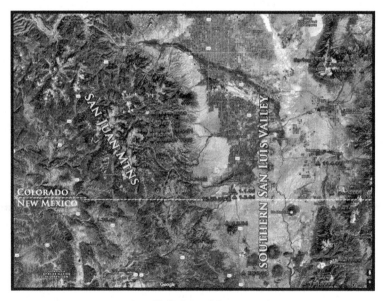

Sightings Map

Historical Reports and Identifying Epicenters of Activity

Obviously, the best place to begin is at the beginning, so let's first take a look at some of the indigenous traditions relating to hairy hominids.

According to the plains dwelling Cheyenne, who were one of 13 tribes that visited the San Luis Valley (SLV) during the warmer months, *Maxemistas* are large, hairy humanoid, bigfoot-like creatures, only they sport birdlike feet. The name Maxemista literally means "big monster" or "big spirit being." Although Maxemistas are considered to be powerful and dangerous creatures, they are also said to be shy and reclusive, unlike the aggressive cannibal dwarves reported in the region for generations. Maxemistas were probably the same "Hairy Men" mentioned in several Cheyenne creation myths. These beings were said to live in caves to the south in the Cheyenne's Front Range Colorado hunting grounds, and they were notable for their shaggy body hair and lack of clothing. Maxemista literally means "Big Elder Brother." Most Cheyenne stories that mention the Hairy Men indicate the Indians regarded the creatures as almost extinct. The Cheyenne Hairy Men Clan or *Hevhaitanio* are said by some to have been named in honor of the Maxemistas.

Blanca Peak

Maxemista are reminiscent of the *Chiye-Tanka*, which are large, shaggy woodland beings of Lakota folklore. Like the other Plains Indians that visited the SLV, the Cheyenne, Arapaho and Kiowa, all have traditions that tell of large, hairy hominids in their environment. There also appear to be similarities to the *Dine'Nakani* that are said to be cannibalistic hairy giants. A major center of sighting reports, the Blanca Peak region of the Sangres is said by the Navajo to be *sisnajiinii*, or the "black sash medicine belt," the place where "all thought originates." I was told by a Navajo medicine man the actual doorways or locations that lead to another realm are not static, they move up and down the range and can be found between Blanca Peak in the south and Crestone Peak to the north.

Pueblo Indians who journeyed to the SLV also have traditions that tell of large, hairy, human-like beings that lived in the remote wilderness. Both the Hopi and the Zuni (North America's aboriginal people) have stories about bigfoot-like creatures. As you travel up the Rio Grande River to Taos—location of the oldest continuously inhabited dwelling in America: The Taos Pueblo—on the northern horizon is North America's largest free-standing mountain, San Antone Peak, located just south of the Colorado border in extreme northern Taos County.

San Antone Mountain

According to the Tewa, San Antone Peak is the "home of Massaaw," the Pueblo Indian "God-of-Death," or in some versions "Creator's" second-in-command. He is usually found underground in the lava tubes where he lives under San Antone Peak, but he does come up above ground from time-to-time. When he is seen on the surface, he is described as being unusually tall, large boned and hairy. And he smells really bad. There are varying stories along this theme, but most stories agree he is mostly benign, but can turn dangerous if surprised or threatened. It should be noted that seven reports were filed by witnesses located on the CO/NM border during the winter of 1994-95, and all occurred within sight of San Antone Peak.

The Hopi elders say the increasing appearances of Bigfoot are not only a message or warning to the individuals or communities to whom he appears, but to humankind at large.... they see Bigfoot as "a messenger who appears in evil times as a warning from the Creator that man's disrespect for His sacred instructions has upset the harmony and balance of existence." To the Hopi, the "big hairy man" is just one form the messenger can take.

When the Independence Gold Mine first began operations around the turn-of-the-century, large human-looking footprints near the entrance were said to have been found by miners, seven miles south of Crestone, Colorado in the Southern Sangre De Cristo Mountains. Sean, a lifelong valley resident and local tracker was told by his grandfather, who worked at the mine, that the men had seen a Bigfoot one night in the late 1920s. According to the tracker, many locals at the time also caught a glimpse of the creature and named it "Boji." The men left food and other treats out for the creature who may have lurked about the camp for several seasons.

Sightings of this ilk appear to have been rare in the southern Rocky Mountains, but the hesitance of locals to come forward during the flurry of encounters in 1994-95, illustrates why it may be so difficult to investigate encounters with these creatures that apparently lurk in the southern Rockies.

Conejos Canyon Summer Range

A series of sightings investigated by BFRO investigator Keith Foster occurred along the upper Conejos River in the early 1990s. One report was filed by by a family that vacationed during the summer months up near the Lake Fork Ranch.

"In 1990, my parents saw a large (7 to 8 foot tall) black, furry creature standing near one of the cabins in the area, as they drove into the Lake Fork Ranch at approximately 1:30 in the afternoon. The creature's head was level with the awning on the porch of the cabin, 8 foot above the ground [from] where it was standing. They at first thought it was a bear standing on its hind legs on the porch, but as they got closer they realized that it was in front of the cabin and on the ground. The creature then ran downhill and across a stream and into the forest out of sight. They were not close enough to it to see any detailed features, only that it was tall, black, and ran on its hind legs. My father looked for tracks, but because of the rocky nature of the ground he found only one relatively good track near the stream. He said the track was about 17" to 18" long and the toes were distinct and humanlike. The great toe was about as large as the bare heel track of a man."

"In 1991, my cousin had his large RV almost tipped over in the night, with him in it, as something grabbed the RV, and rocked it violently. He stayed up the rest of the night, with pistol in hand. In the morning a box of apples was missing, box and all. In 1995, through casual conversation with some campers at the nearby Lake Fork Campground, that something had rocked another RV, in the night. I submit this report in hopes that other Colorado incidents will come to light... The Colorado Springs newspapers carried an article a few years back."

The sightings along the Lake Fork of the Conejos ceased in 1992 and 1993, but more sighting reports would return in 1997 and in 2009.

Maasaw on the Prowl?

December, 1993, the New Mexico-Colorado Border:

During a seven-day period, from the last week of December into the first week of January, seven "Bigfoot" encounters were reported to local Costilla County, Colorado authorities. These encounters were all reported within a seven-mile area, and because of local's reluctance to go on record, I've not pinpointed the exact location of these alleged events. Many area residents appear to be very protective of the occasionally seen "Bigfoot," not to mention sensitive to their own privacy. The following events were related to me by the Conejos County undersheriff.

Several days before, a niece of the undersheriff called to tell him that "she had found some tracks that he'd better come look at." She described them as being huge, human-looking, barefoot tracks. Not taking it too seriously, he didn't immediately investigate. On the morning of the 31st, he followed her to the remote location with a video camera to document the scene. He wished he had gone out the day she called, for what she showed him was incredible.

Descending for hundreds of yards down a cow trail were two sets of human-looking tracks. One measured 20 inches, the other 18 inches long. They descended over a variety of terrain: rocks, snow and bare ground. They were unmistakable. One of the larger prints was so pristine that "you could see toenail marks!" I have seen the footage of these tracks and visited the site, and there is no mistaking the classic Bigfoot tracks. Shaquille O'Neal would be the smaller one's baby brother. Shaq has a size 20 foot, these tracks were a size 35 to 40!

The undersheriff's niece also related a strange story. On the eve of discovering the tracks, she had heard her dog barking furiously outside. She went out to see why he was barking when she heard huge "footsteps go running by the house." Outside she found her dog cowering inside the fenced yard. The dog had been locked out of the yard. She put him back outside the fence. A short time later, he started barking again, and once more she heard the huge running footsteps and "a twang of something hitting the barb wire fence." She went back outside and found her dog shaking inside the fence once again!

The following morning while stalking a herd of deer to take photos, she happened to stumble on two sets of giant, barefoot tracks walking side-by-side. She called her uncle to report the possible encounter and the tracks. The investigating officers noted that drops of blood seemed to accompany the larger of the two sets of tracks in the trackway. Subsequent testing by the Colorado State Crime Lab indicated the blood samples were from an elk.

The undersheriff related several other recent reports from that seven-day time-period. One encounter found a mother and son driving back from the mountains just after sunset. As they rounded a curve, their headlights revealed a creature covered in hair with large glowing eyes and pointed ears in the middle of the road. The mother slammed on her brakes. Not knowing what to do, with the thing blocking their way, she put the car in reverse and backed up. This evidently scared the thing, for "it dropped down on all fours and ran away like a dog!"

They proceeded directly to the sheriff's office to report what they had seen. According to the undersheriff, "They were real upset about it." This impressed the authorities enough for them to mount a search for the creature. They combed the hills but found no sign of it.

One interesting correlation to the above, during this same two-day period, a Washington State man reported seeing a Bigfoot with large pointed ears and wings near Mount Rainier.

Motorists who spotted large, hairy humanoid creatures, at night, next to Highway 285, subsequently filed two additional reports. A trucker who claimed the one he saw was "all white" made one of the reports.

Yet another report was filed by a man who claimed he witnessed a pair of Bigfoot "stalking a herd of elk" on the northern side of San Antone Mountain. He was close enough to see them "signaling to each other" while watching them through his binoculars.

These types of witnessed accounts have also been filed by trained observers. A New Mexico Cattle Inspector, also an ex-military member, who lives in Rancho de Taos, New Mexico, told me he watched with binoculars, "a white Bigfoot" clamor up the rocky slope of a firecut during the late fall of 1993. It ascended the seemingly impossible terrain in less than 30 minutes. He really became impressed with the creature's apparent agility when he tried to make the same climb the following day. It took him "over two hours."

Blanca Peak Encounter

Lilly Lake is located high up in the Blanca Massif. The Blanca Peak area is rich with historical references to Bigfoot-type creatures. Completely surrounded by 14,000-foot high mountains, the lake is nestled in at above 11,000 feet. Lilly Lake is also where, believe-it-or-not, two fishermen in 1966 reported seeing a "platypus" scurry into the lake and swim away. In the mid-1980s a "white buffalo" was reported standing by the lake edge. The witness claimed it vanished from sight "in a flash of light."

The springtime 1994 Bigfoot encounter that follows occurred

within a mile of the common intersection of Huerfano, Alamosa, and Costilla counties. It is also located about two miles from a summer 2000 sighting over near Como Lake, just over the mountain saddle in Alamosa County. The encounter was roughly 1/3 of a mile down hill from the lake and 1/3 of a mile to the west, off the trail and down into the trees. The witness gave BFRO investigators the following account:

"I have a biology degree and work as a wildlife biologist. I usually don't tell people about it, but after reading some other stories on your web page -why not. [The witness was able to supply exact coordinates, A & G References: T28s R73w, sec 24, SE 1/4, N1/2. 6th principle meridian.] The sighting occurred approximately 4 - 6 pm.

I was with a group of friends hiking up to a mountain lake called Lilly Lake on Blanca Peak. It was a weekday, overcast, evening. The light conditions were good, not bright or dark — but it was overcast...

After hanging out at the lake we had all started to turn back. After a while we decided to race down the hill off the trail back to camp. (last one there was cooking). I hung back with another friend to just walk back and carry people's gear.

Shortly after everyone took off like a bat out of hell, we saw something jump between two trees. The figure was stretched out like someone doing a jumping-jack while jumping in a lunge. It must have been at least 6 feet tall. At first we thought it was my brother messing with us, he was the only one in our group tall enough. Both my friend and I have a lot of outdoor experience. It was positively not a deer, sheep, elk or a bear. Although it's color was very similar to the light grey of a mule deer during that time of year. The arms were clearly visible as were the legs, but it moved very fast between the trees.

It was very unusual that we never heard a sound come from the animal. It was only about 30-60 yards away and we didn't hear a thing! We are both very experienced with wildlife and the sounds of the different animals.

[There was] one other witness. Just prior to the sighting the whole group of six were hiking back to camp. Four of the others had just ran through the timber before us."

The witness said he was "surprised at the lack of sound from the movement of the animal. Neither padded footfalls like bear, nor hoofed footfalls like deer, elk, or sheep. No sound at all." He reported his encounter in 2009.

The following reports also occurred during that spring of 1994, but were located across the valley to the southwest, up near the headwaters of the Conejos River—located along the Lake Fork, Conejos County, Colorado, near the border with the San Juan Wilderness.

"In the first week of June, 1994, my 2 sons and I were fishing in a beaver pond on the Lake Fork of the Conejos about 1 mile upstream from where the Lake Fork of the Conejos meets with the Conejos River. It was near sunset and the sun had already gone behind the mountains. There was a sparsely forested rise toward the southwest, above the beaver pond we were fishing. Just beyond this rise was the south slope of a ridge of old growth forest.

A horrible gravelly scream or yell of almost unbelievable volume came from just inside the forest at about 150 to 200 yards distance. I am an avid bowhunter of 20 years experience with all manner of big game and the sound was definitely not an elk or bear. Elk make some loud and unusual sounds but this sound was vastly different and many times louder. I noticed that a light breeze was blowing from us toward the source of the sound. If the creature had a good sense of smell, it probably smelled us. Bowhunting experience has taught me that an elk would smell us under the same conditions. The sound had a threatening essence to it. The sound itself was kind of indescribable and seemed louder than a creature could possibly make.

Whatever made the two tone scream must have one big set of lungs and a very large, megaphone-size mouth. The sound lasted about 1 or 2 seconds and was repeated three times, with a 10 or 15 second pause between each blast of noise. I was unarmed and decided since I had my sons with me I would give the creature its space. We left.

I was somewhat alarmed, but would have gone to the source of the sound if I had not had my sons with me. I did go to the area of the source of the sound the next morning alone at sunrise to see if I could find tracks or other evidence of the source of the sound.

I [found] some very old large tracks in soft dirt on a flat area about 1/2 mile uphill. They were about 16" by 8" in size but too old to discern any toes or other detail and could have been bear tracks distorted and enlarged by rains and time. There was a line of about 20 of these large tracks in single file across the bare ground of this bench. Most of the rest of the soil in this area is too rocky to see the tracks of soft-footed animals well. The tracks I found were at least a week or two old. I spent all morning looking the area over, hoping to find evidence, but hoping I didn't find the creature itself."

Another report was filed from a witness further downstream, out toward Fox Creek where the sighting of the pointed eared bigfoot was made by the mother and her son on December 25, 1993:

"In 1996 my children and I backpacked to Big Lake and spent 4 uneventful nights in a backpacking tent. Big lake is within 1/2 mile of where the other reports for Conejos County occurred. We watched one of the creatures for 5 minutes in the summer of 1997. We did not go to the area this year because of lack of vacation time. I know that this group of sasquatches are following the herds of elk in the area and that they are migrating south and east of the Conejos County summer area to lower elevations with the elk herds. Interestingly, these are the same herds of elk that summer in the Lake Fork area of the Conejos. I did find an area where the game animals would not go in the area, in spite of good browse and grazing. The area is, I think, home base in the summer for these creatures."

Again the following summer, the week of July 13, 1997, additional sightings on the Lake Fork of the Conejos were filed by area residents and visitors. This next event occurred on the Lake Fork foot trail, about half way between Big Lake and Rock Lake. The sighting was made from the eastern branch of the Saddle Creek logging road [and was] line-of-sight distance approximately 2.5 miles SSE of Platoro, Colorado.

"I was on the logging road, about 0.25 miles lateral and 1,000 ft or so vertical distance from the Lake Fork trail when I made the sighting. We were standing on a rocky overlook next to the logging road which allowed a good view of the Lake Fork Valley, including Big Lake and Rock Lake.

It was approximately 1:30 in the afternoon. [There were] clear skies with unlimited visibility. The sunlight was shining directly on the Lake Fork Valley floor [and I] had a clear view with no obstructions. The Valley floor was about 0.5 miles away and 1000 or 1500 feet downhill. The overlook from which my wife and I were watching is about two miles in an easterly direction from where the Saddle Creek logging road forks off to the Tobacco Lake trailhead.

I saw with binoculars a group of three hikers and a dog making their way down the Lake Fork Trail toward the Lake Fork Ranch. They were walking at a fairly normal speed. What I would say to be 400 or 500 yards in front of them was a large, black object moving in the same direction — away from the hikers— at a much faster speed. It was not on the trail, but instead in the meadow next to the trail. It seemed as if it was spooked by the hikers. I'd say it was about a half mile from me, and 1000 or so feet downhill, so I couldn't get a really good gauge on how big it was. Although, judging its size against the hikers, it was clearly much larger than a man. There is no question that it was bipedal; not once did I see it move [as a] quadruped. This was definitely not a bear.

As it appeared from my vantage point, I don't think the hikers ever had a direct view of this thing. The clearing in which the hikers were was separated from the clearing across which it was running by a tongue of aspens growing down into the valley. I watched for about 5 minutes as it moved away from the hikers, eventually jumping Lake Fork and bearing farther away from the trail and disappearing into the trees on the southern edge of the valley. Are there any other reports in this area? I've been going to the Conejos for about 25 years, and have never seen or heard of anything like this.

Nothing was heard during the incident. I travelled down the logging road soon after watching this to see if I could intercept the hikers, but couldn't find a car or anything at the base of the trail."

The following report was submitted to BFRO by the primary witness on September 24, 2000. The alleged sighting event occurred four days earlier in the Sangre De Cristo Mountains on Sunday, August 20th, 2000. If you travel west from Walsenberg, CO taking U.S. 160 westbound up and over La Veta Pass and go through the towns of Ft. Garland and Blanca, and turn right on CO 150. You are headed north toward the Great Sand Dunes. The huge stack of mountains on your right is called the Blanca Massif. Go about 2 miles on 150 and turn on what is called Lake Como Road. This is called "the toughest Four Wheel Drive Road in Colorado, and the third toughest in the U.S." Take the road (up & over "Oil pan Rock" until it ends at a small parking area a quarter mile below the lake, that is 6.8 miles from the road's trailhead below. It will take you about 4 hours.

The sighting event had an innocent beginning. The primary witness with his mother, father and an uncle were four-wheeling up the Como Lake Road:

"We had made it past Lake Como and to the end of the Jeep road … [where] the forest opens up into a meadow, it is about 11,000 to 11,500 feet at about timberline … [This is] where we fished for a while and ate our lunch … When we saw the creature it was about 1:40 p.m. It was cloudy, and starting to drizzle rain.

Prior to the incident, on our way up about 11:30 a.m. and on our way back we smelled what seemed like celery in the exact same place …

When we left the last lake, it was about 1:30 p.m., with my uncle and me in the lead on our four-wheelers. We had gone about a half a mile when my uncle and I both spotted something that looked like a dead, burned tree stump that was about 7 to 8 feet tall …

We didn't think too much of it until it moved. It stood upright and walked like a man. At first, we thought it was a hiker but it was all the same color, from head to toe. It walked about 15 yards before it walked into the trees. My uncle and I both stopped to make sure we saw the same thing. But we drove down the road about 300 to 400 yards before we decided to go look for it. We walked into the trees about 200 yards and came to a small meadow. My uncle was looking the other way when at the other end of the meadow it ran through. I yelled, "There it goes"!

We took off after it, on foot. This time I got a little bit better chance to look at it. The creature was a light to a medium brown and had shaggy long hair, it stood about 7 feet tall … forest opens up into a meadow, it is about 11,000 to 11,500 feet or at about timberline. Where we decided to chase the creature down, there was a big flat rock about 100 feet long and kind of stuck out of the bank …

When we reached the end of the meadow, each of us went in an opposite direction. My uncle went the same direction as the bigfoot, and I went the other way in case it double-backed on us. But we didn't see the creature after that. We did find a few footprints, but didn't have any plaster to make a mold. So we went back down the mountain. I know what I saw that day and no one can tell us otherwise."

BFRO investigators noted in their report: "The witness said when the animal crossed the meadow in front of him, it was only 15 [to] 20 yards away. He said the animal was swinging its long arms and moving in "either a fast walk or a slow run," but it "didn't bend its knees much." The witness also noted the animal's long fur appeared to be "matted."

Now we have to swing west, over La Magna Pass and head toward the infamous Jicarilla Apache town of Dulce, New Mexico—located on the Apache Reservation where it straddles the Colorado/New Mexico border. Headed west, just before you head into Dulce on NM State Highway 64, you come to the intersection of 64 and Highway 84, which begins at 64 and heads north to Chromo, CO and then up to Pagosa Springs, CO.

The two witnesses, like most of our region's reports, were driving when they had their sighting experience.

"It was Friday, January 25, 2001. At first I was not even going to go down to the area where I and a friend saw a bigfoot. I was going to finish watching the Pagosa Basketball team play and go home. But a boxing match was on the same night and my best friend's (not the friend that saw it with me) brother-in-law was going to buy it on Pay per View, and his brother-in-law lives in the area of Cromo and Edith, Colorado. There are always some crazy sightings of UFO's and Bigfoot sightings. I really didn't believe in these type of things until I saw one for myself.

We watched the boxing match and after it was over we started to head back to Pagosa Springs on Cromo Road, and we were almost to Highway 84 when about 20 yards in front of us this thing or bigfoot crossed and went quickly, almost as if we were seeing things. I didn't know what to think, so I asked Sammy if he saw it, and he said, "what was that?" We got up to where it crossed and I opened my door to look down on the road and saw a foot print and Sammy opened his door and saw a track too. We both freaked out and I drove as fast as I could to Pagosa Springs. We didn't tell that many people, only the ones that would believe us."

Follow-up investigation report by BFRO Investigator Dr. Steven Coy:

I interviewed this young man one morning at a Denny's restaurant, and have since talked to him on the phone on at least one occasion. He is an avid outdoorsman and hunter, having been raised, as I recall, in the Pagosa Springs area though he no longer lives there.

I have no doubts whatsoever as to his credibility, and subsequently met and interviewed, at his suggestion, a former high school teacher who knows the witness well. This teacher has also talked to one or more additional individuals who have had some kind of sighting or encounter in this Pagosa Springs area.

When asked about the size of the creature, the witness stated that he believed it had to be at least eight feet tall, perhaps nine, as it smoothly crossed the county road in approximately one and one half strides.

Our next encounter occurred in January 2007, in the Sangre de Cristo Mountains right below the Colorado-New Mexico border in northern Taos County. Right below the border is the small hamlet of Costilla, New Mexico. If you turn to the east and head in toward the Sangre de Cristo Mountains, after a couple of miles you'll hit a curve in the road. Right off to your left, just over the hill in the pasture, is some sort of doorway. Over the years, locals traveling along the road to Costilla have witnessed strange sightings of darting aerial craft, and there are stories of entities that appear to emerge through some sort of doorway or portal. Now stories of this type are practically impossible to confirm, but there does appear to be something going on just off the road to Costilla.

"Interesting find becomes scary experience for Costilla man" read the headline of the *Taos News* on Thursday, January 18, 2007. The story, written by Jerry A. Padilla was picked up by the wire services and flit around the Internet and the world like wildfire. I attempted several times to track down the primary witness, but was unsuccessful. With all the instant notoriety, I'm not surprised. What makes this report even more intriguing is that a couple of months later in late February 2007, a set of huge, humanoid tracks were observed traveling through the snow for hundreds of yards from near the Padilla sighting location, north over the New Mexico border—headed toward Wild Horse Mesa in Colorado. This is a notorious site of other Bigfoot reports from the late 1970s and early 1980s. The following is from Padilla's *Taos News* article:

"Arturo 'Homie' Martinez, 67, of Costilla [agreed] to tell the *Taos News* about my experience because many people I've shared the information with don't seem to take me serious. However many do, and they have encouraged me to come forward with my story."

Martinez, originally of Arroyo Hondo, has spent a lifetime in the mountains, canyons and wilds of northern New Mexico and southern Colorado, and can identify all the native wildlife, plants and animals, whatever the season or conditions. Not long ago, he and a person he calls a "super friend" had a frightening, but very interesting experience while scouting for elk in preparation for a hunt. His friend has chosen to remain anonymous.

Martinez made personal notes about what happened in this mountain canyon area Sept. 27. "I, myself, and my friend set out to scout for game, but something weird happened."

He explained that earlier the first day, while scouting in stands of aspens within sight of the community of Amalia from up high, Martinez found an interesting, naturally formed piece of aspen tree that strongly resembled a human face. "Nobody carved it, it grew that way and I decided to bring it back."

After leaving the object at home, Martinez and friend returned to another area several miles away from where they had been earlier in the day. This time, while driving on another fork of the rough road, they found many tops of aspen trees cleanly broken off that were strewn over the road. "We decided to investigate who was breaking the trees and throwing them on the road. I asked my friend, "Who would want to do this?" Martinez explained, "These were aspens ranging in size from 3 to 4 inches to 6 to 8 inches in diameter, cleanly broken about 13 to 15 feet up the trunk of the trees. There were no tracks of bear or elk, or human tracks — no tracks of any kind, no sawdust at the bottom of the trees and what was strange, it was as if they were thrown several feet away from where they were broken. There were two big aspens completely uprooted and thrown away from where they had been growing. If bears had broken them, they would have left claw marks. Bears leave a smell on trees they scratch or break. Elk in rutting battles leave the ground very disturbed. It wasn't, and seeing many broken trees we continued on to investigate who or what was breaking them. The broken treetops were lying in the road as if something or someone wanted to say, "Nobody is welcome here." Rounding a curve, my tire blew out and things started getting very scary," he continued.

"We could hear elk bugling up higher and we decided to walk back down since it was late afternoon," Martinez said. "We needed to get a spare, and come back to change the tire. We were taking our time checking out more broken trees, and there was easily over a 100 broken the same way. That's when I heard the scariest noise I have ever heard in my life."

"It started at first, sounding like an elk bugling, then turned into a scary roar so loud it kept echoing through the canyon," he continued. "The elk up high stopped bugling. It kept making that noise at us, it reminded me of the noise the devil made in the Exorcist movie. Whatever was making the noise started breaking trees and throwing them in our direction a few seconds later."

"Then I saw a huge creature moving through the edge of an aspen grove, about 30 to 40 feet from me. It walked upright, but hunched over, maybe 6 feet tall bent over, and standing straight was 7 to 8 feet tall with very dark fur all over. It was not a bear. Bears don't walk like humans. I am convinced I saw what many call Sasquatch. Even with my gun, I was very scared and we left in a hurry. It seemed to be following in the edge of the trees, breaking more, throwing them toward us and making that awful noise. It was almost dark and we had to get out of there," he recounted.

The two men fled down the mountain, and Martinez said every time the creature roared the noise continued reverberating through the entire area. "I felt like at any moment something was going to grab me from behind all the way out of there."

They arrived on foot in Costilla well after dark, deciding no matter how scared they felt, it was necessary to return to the canyon, change the blown tire and bring Martinez's vehicle back.

The two men returned to where the vehicle was parked, and by the time they changed the spare it was after 2 a.m. on Sept. 28.

"We decided to stay until daylight and try to find out what it really was we had experienced," Martinez continued, "It was deathly quiet the whole time, nothing moving, no elk bugling, not a sound at all. At sunrise we checked around, found more aspens broken the same way. Nothing else happened to us. There was no sign of anything out of the ordinary except more broken trees."

Not finding any other evidence of their frightening experience of the afternoon before, Martinez and his friend returned home.

"Like I said, I know what I saw. I know it is not a bear or any other of the wildlife I have seen around here all my life. I decided to tell my story because America, wake up, these creatures exist," he said. "Every time I go into the mountains anywhere from now on I will have a camera and an audio recorder with me. I have had other people tell me that even though they wish to remain anonymous; they have had similar experiences over the years, but don't say much because they get ridiculed. I know what I saw and heard."

Almost 12 years later, after over a decade of no official reports in the Conejos River/Lost Fork region, a new report was filed by a hunter on a four-wheeler:

"In early June of this year [2009] I was riding my four-wheeler above Jasper, CO. I heard a loud howling noise. There was no wind that day, and I could not focus in on the source. I had seen a lot of sheep on Cornwall Mountain on the way up so I figured it was a dog or the sheepherder. When I had finished my water, I was loading everything back on the bike, when I heard the same sound again, only this time it was much louder. I zeroed in on it and my heart stopped!

"Slightly below my logging road and to my right, I observed a very large dirty black man-like creature with his hands around an aspen tree. It was leaning a little to the right and staring at me. I stood very still and never took my eyes off of it. After about seven or eight minutes it turned and simply walked off down the hill. I will add that I am a 30-year archery hunter, and have successfully tagged bears in this same [hunting] unit. This was no bear. It was large and shaggy looking."

He added that he had heard of sightings on the Tobacco Lake trail, which is about six or so miles south of here, over at the Lake Fork of the Conejos River.

Later that same Fall on November 3, 2009, across the valley in Costilla County—right at the Sanchez Reservoir, another report was filed by an elk hunter investigated by BFRO Investigator Dennis Pfohl:

"It was evening time around 5:00 p.m., it was cold with snow on the ground as it had just finished snowing. I was looking through binoculars scanning for elk and saw what I thought was a man walking down the path on the mountain. [I] thought it was unusual [that] he didn't have any hunter orange on. It then turned sideways and I noticed it was bigger than a normal man. [It was] walking with a long gait and was brown—almost the color of elk fur. [It] was walking on two feet rather fast. It walked to the ridge and looked over [the] valley, then walked up the same path it came in on. It was clearly visible because of snow in background. Then it disappeared."

Pfohl spoke to the witness, Freddie, over the phone and he added the following additional information to his original report:

"Freddie is an experienced dozer and heavy equipment operator in the coal industry and lives in Alabama. He has been to Colorado twice in the past few years to hunt elk and deer during rifle season, and he stated he is a life-long experienced hunter.

On November 4th of 2009 he was in Colorado hunting with some friends on private property near the Sanchez Reservoir in south central Colorado. It had been snowing most of that day and about six inches of snow had accumulated on the ground.

While glassing the surrounding area with binoculars in the late afternoon hours, approximately one half hour before sunset, and while looking for elk, Freddie noticed a tall figure walking along a ridgeline below him and to his southeast. It was approximately 300-400 yards from his location. He thought it was an elk at first and then realized it was walking on two legs like a man. To him the figure looked large and tall, and was covered in light brown, long, flowing hair. He watched as it moved along the ridgeline, all the while facing away from his direction and acting as if it was looking for something towards a clearing to it's east. It never left the tree line. He stated that he thinks the distance it covered while it approached and left was between 50-60 yards each way and it covered it quickly. It then turned back walking in the direction it approached and quickly disappeared back into the trees.

He then thought, "What kind of idiot would be out walking in this area without hunters orange on and to possibly get shot?" Freddie stated that despite his thoughts, he knew that it was not a man.

Freddie did not want to trespass on the surrounding private property to get a closer look—instead he chose to go back to his group."

Dennis Pfohl is a business owner in Colorado and an avid Outdoorsman. He attended the 2004 New Mexico Expedition (Mescalero IR), 2005 New Mexico Expedition (Mescalero), 2005 California Sierras Expedition, 2005/2008 Oklahoma Expedition and the 2008 Texas Expedition. He was organizer of the first Colorado

BFRO Expedition in 2005, and organized numerous additional Colorado Bigfoot Expeditions.

Red River Canyon, New Mexico

The following July 9, 2009 account was investigated by BFRO Investigator Todd Perteet. A couple visiting the Red River Canyon region, located straight east from the town of Questa, New Mexico had awoken before dawn to hitch up their travel trailer and start their journey back home to Oklahoma. They had parked their traveler several yards from the Red River in the heavily wooded terrain that ran along the creek. There were steep mountainous cliffs all around them. The woman had gotten up first and then the man arose and went into the bathroom. It was about 5:00 AM on a clear morning.

"My wife opened the door and said that someone was standing outside the entry door to the bedroom of the trailer. I went back to the room and saw a large shadow in the window. The window is privacy glass so they couldn't see inside. I could see a chest, a head and about half of the arm. I reached into the night stand and took out my pistol thinking that it was someone. I then started toward the back of the trailer to the main entry door.

While I was doing this, my wife thought to take photos. She took three photos which does show the shadow of whatever it was very well. When I was at the other end of the trailer I opened the door and turned on the outside light at the same time. There was nothing there, I did hear what sounded like someone walking very quickly in the distance. I went around the trailer but couldn't see anyone.

It was at this time that I realized that the window on the door is too high for someone to have been standing there. I took pictures to show how high it is. We waited until daylight to go back outside, I looked around the front and side of the trailer and noticed what appeared to be large tracks in the gravel. I took pictures of these.

My friend who is a photographer took a copy of the pictures showing the shadow in the window and enlarged them while trying to keep the clarity and it is possible to make out some of the features. His exact words are "it kind of looks like Harry from Harry and the Hendersons." I don't know what it was but it was very strange and the photos are quite interesting."

Perteet did a follow up interview and determined the following additional facts about the couple's experience with the large hairy hominid.

They had spent six nights at the same location and had not noticed anything unusual prior to this incident. When he opened the back door, he did not see anyone else outside but did hear dogs barking in the adjacent trailer. Their trailer was in the last (west) space on the row. The figure appeared on the west side of their bedroom so it wouldn't have been between two trailers.

Figure was somewhat backlit by a street light near a building approximately 200-250 feet to the west/northwest of their location. The creature did not make any noises while at the window. The step below the bedroom door was retracted and no movement was felt in the trailer, which would indicate the visitor was standing on the ground, not the step. There was also nothing else nearby to stand on. Measured height from the ground to the top of the window (where figure was photographed) is eight feet. Glass pane is sixteen inches wide by twenty-four inches high.

Track observed, closest to the trailer, was approximately three feet away. The reason for photographing the figure was that she believed it was possibly somebody that meant them harm. She also noted that it was so strange to see someone standing at the window. There were numerous other people in RV's occupying the campground and they did not tell anyone at the campground of their experience.

On the night of February 20, 2011, a couple driving home to Colorado had a sighting encounter near Tres Piedras, New Mexico. They had just left the intersection of NM Highway 64 that heads SE to Taos, where there is a blinking red light on Highway 285, the road which carried them the final 40 miles to their home in Antonito, CO. The report was filed with BFRO by the witness's daughter and was investigated by Ron Martinez.

The sighting occurred just north from the flashing light of Tres Piedras, "right where there is a wall of rocks on each side of the road." When "a big, tall, black human-looking thing which stood over six feet tall, very husky, walked very fast like a gorilla [would] walk across the road. The thing popped out from the east side of road 285 crossing to the west side. It was a very scary situation according to my parents. They suggest that anybody, especially female drivers to please be careful!"

Martinez spoke with the husband first and he described the biped's height as 7-8 feet tall. Witness estimated its weight at around 400-500 pounds. It was black in color and he stated its arms were as long as his (the witness') legs. "It moved like a gorilla," he said. He was surprised he didn't hit it with his vehicle. He thought it crossed the road east to west in about "one leap." It never faced them so they didn't get a look at its face. Witness stated it seemed not to be concerned as they drove by heading north at about 55mph.

Martinez then spoke with the wife who saw it first, alerting her husband who was driving. Her description was consistent with her husband's. Since the sighting, she describes the creature she saw to others as looking like a "caveman or Bigfoot".

Eight months later, on October 14, 2011, a "25-year veteran of the Colorado Department of Corrections and his son were on their way to go elk hunting near La Veta Pass (located about 25 miles east of the town of Ft. Garland.) The location off of Colorado State Highway 160 where the sighting occurred is a popular spot for elk to cross the highway. They were headed west when they witnessed the human-like creature: The corrections officer and his son both witnessed a bipedal figure crossing the road from Northwest to Southeast (from right to left) at approximately 5 am, a couple of hours before sunrise.

"The figure was bent over and moving very fast, with the arms noticeably pumping. After crossing the highway the figure ran up a steep embankment and went over a four-foot barbed wire fence at the top… the figure was grey and shaggy, with noticeable hair on the forearms. [We] were approximately 40 to 50 yards away when we saw the figure. We were driving and observed a hairy animal run across the road. It was on two legs and running really fast. It had very long hair on its arms. When it crossed the road we stopped and heard whistling in the trees. I have hunted Colorado most of my life."

After the sighting the father and son pulled off the highway in an effort to attempt to determine the identity of the figure. As they were walking around shining a flashlight along the crossing path they heard two distinct whistles.

According to BFRO investigator Kevin Burns, who did the follow up interview with the witnesses: "The witness mentioned that this stretch of highway is a common elk crossing point. It has been noted in many previous reports that Sasquatches hunt not only deer but also various ungulates such as elk. Hearing whistling sounds is also common and is often speculated to be a method of communication or alert."

Final Thoughts:

What do we know about Bigfoot in the Southern Rocky Mountains? Besides the before-mentioned fact there seem to be less sighting reports than one would expect in such a remote, mountainous, sparsely populated part of the country? Well first off, it appears all sighting events are centered around areas of the semi-desert terrain that have water. With the exception of the wintertime sightings around San Antone Mountain, this is probably the most obvious fact that jumps out from sighting proximate data. These creatures, like all animals, require water to survive and Bigfoot is no different.

From the official reports, it would appear they have a preference for Sangre de Cristo Creek, which flows down from La Veta Pass west towards Ft. Garland; the upper and lower sections of the Conejos River, as it flows out of the San Juan Mountains down into the San Luis Valley, where it merges with the Rio Grande. During the summer months the Lilly and Winchell Lakes region, located high up in the saddle between the five peaks of the Blanca Massif, and in the Red River region in the Sangre de Cristo Mountains—east of Questa—west of the Moreno Valley.

San Juans

Another major center of activity is around Dulce, New Mexico on the Jicarilla Apache Reservation. Space restraints won't allow for a detailed accounting of sighting activity in this region, but my investigation has uncovered possibly hundreds of sightings in the area. Ex Department of Public Safety Chief Hoyt Velarde has told me about the many reports he investigated in his over 30 years on the force—including several close encounters he personally experienced. In the next issue of Wood Knocks I'll attempt to put the Jicarilla encounters into focus, and list the events that have officially been reported by the Apache and others in the area.

Bigfoot Reports from Central Southern Colorado/Northern New Mexico

In the Footsteps of the Indian Yeti

by Richard Freeman

The expeditionary team of Dr Chris Clark, Adam Davies, Dave Archer and myself, who had previously searched for the Russian almasty (a relic hominid) and the puzzling Sumatra orang-pendek (mystery ape), were getting our heads together in planning where to go on the official Centre for Fortean Zoology (CFZ) expedition in 2010.

Several years before Adam had been in Tibet on the track of the yeti. Ian Redmond, Tropical Field Biologist and Conservationist, mentioned to him there were numerous reports of the yeti in the northern Indian state of Meghalaya. Upon returning to England he investigated more closely and found that a local documentary film maker and journalist, Dipu Marak had been on the trail of the creature for some years.

I too had heard of the Indian yeti or as it is locally known *'mande-burung,'* the forest man. In June of 2008 BBC journalist Alistair Lawson visited the area to investigate sightings of the creature. He was impressed by the remote, undisturbed landscape and wrote…

"If ever there was terrain where a peace-loving yeti could live its life undisturbed by human interference, then this has surely got to be it. Perhaps the most famous reported sighting was in April 2002, when forestry officer James Marak was among a team of 14 officials carrying out a census of tigers in Balpakram when they saw what they thought was a yeti."

Dipu had given the BBC some hairs he had found at a remote

area called Balpakram. Upon analysis these proved to be from a *Nemorhaedus goral*, a species of Asian wild goat. This however did not negate the eyewitness reports.

We decided that the CFZ team should investigate and began to lay plans for a trip to India. Adam, who is a great organizer, contacted Dipu who in turn organized guides, lodges and contact with eyewitnesses.

The four of us were to be joined on this trip by Jonathan McGowen. Jon is an excellent field naturalist and taxidermist as well as being the curator of the Bournemouth Natural History Museum.

On Halloween 2010 we flew out to India. We arrived in the mad cacophony that is Delhi in the evening and checked into our hotel.

The following day we flew out from the surprisingly clean and efficient Delhi airport to Guwahati in Assam. We were met at Guwahati by our chief guide Rudy Sangma, assistant guide Pintu, and our drivers. We then began the long journey to the town of Tura in the West Garo Hills.

Meghalaya is a mountainous state in the north east of India. It was carved out of the state of Assam in 1972 to accommodate the Khasi, Garo, and Jaintia tribes, who at one time had their own kingdoms. The three territories had come under British administration in the early 1800s and were assimilated into Assam in 1835. Once fierce headhunters, the Garos were among the first Indians to be converted to Christianity by British missionaries. After conversation the tribes were largely left alone allowing a lot of their culture to remain intact.

This expedition was to be somewhat atypical. Generally we camp out in the jungle, mountains, desert or wherever 24 / 7, returning only to 'civilization' to stock up on supplies. This time the Indian Government would not let us stay overnight in the jungle due to the activities of the insurgent group known as the Garo National Liberation Army. This significantly reduced our chances of seeing the mande-burung.

As the winding roads rose upwards, giving way to rocky tracks, Rudy told me of some of the other strange creatures from the folklore of the Garo Hills. One creature that looms large in the Garos is the *sankuni*. This is a monstrous snake that sports a crest upon its head much like a rooster's comb. Sound familiar? It should, the description of the sankuni matches up very well with that of the *naga*, the vast crested serpent I searched for in Thailand, and the *ninki-nanka*, the serpent dragon of the Gambia I hunted in 2006. All are said to have crests, be of huge size, have shining black scales, live in lakes or rivers as well as subterranean burrows, and to have an association with rain. The uncanny dovetailing of these stories made me seriously wonder if the sankuni and other monster serpents are based on encounters with a real-life species of gigantic snake unknown to science. Unlike the naga or ninki-nanka the sankuni is also associated with landslides. Its underground crawling is supposed to cause massive shifts in wet earth. This sounds much like the weird South American serpentine cryptid known as the *minhocão* that is said to cause disruption, uproot trees, destroy houses and even alter the course of rivers. The sankuni is not wholly malevolent. Indeed, in legend, it is said to allow humans to use its great coils as a bridge allowing them to cross rivers. It is also said to manifest in dreams, warning people of impending landslides. The sankuni is said to crow like a rooster much the same as the crested crown cobra of Africa. It's likeness to both the European basilisk (save in vast size) and the giant serpentine lindorms and worms hardly needs to be stated.

Another weird entity from folklore Rudy told me of was the *skaul*. This is a vampiric entity that resembles a normal human being by day, but at night its head detaches from its body and flies about as an independent entity. It has luminous hair and saliva. The skaul is said to feed on excrement and rubbish, but also to suck up human life force, causing the victim to fall ill, weaken and finally die. The skaul may have been an early attempt to explain disease and illness. The luminous hair and saliva might well be based on early sightings of ball lightning or some other meteorological phenomena. The skaul has analogues across Asia with the Malayan *Penanggalan*, the Philippine *Manananggal*, the Balinese *Leyak*, the Thai *Krasue* and the Japanese *Nukekubi*.

We arrived in the ugly mountain town of Tura and met with Dipu Marak, the man who had been on the trail of the mande-burung for many years. A delightful man, Dipu has a deep and infectious passion for the Indian yeti. He told us how he recalled hearing stories of the beast in his childhood and that sparked his lifelong interest. With a Garo mother and a Bengali father, Dipu is a huge fellow who towers over everyone else in the town.

The following day we journeyed to Nokrek National Park. The

hills here are covered by deep virgin rainforest, and we began an arduous trek within it. The terrain was very hilly with a constant climbing up and down of ridges. We came across the nest of a wild boar and climbed down a dangerously steep cliff to investigate a small cave. The cave offered up no results other than the paw prints of a small felid, possibly an Indian leopard cat.

We planted camera traps at several locations making sure each had a good view of the area. All the traps were baited with bananas and oranges. The mande-burung is supposed to be primarily a herbivore, although there are a couple of sightings of the creatures eating freshwater crabs. Dipu told us of one case where a farmer saw a family of four mande-burung stealing pineapples from his fields. The creatures ran away upon seeing him, snatching fruit as they went.

We moved from Tura in the West Garos down to Siju in the South Garos. We were met by Rufus, a friend of Rudy and another guide. We stopped in a rather downheel and basic -but clean- tourist lodge. Close by were the Siju Caves where the village head man had supposedly encountered a mande-burung several years before. The whole area was awash with wildlife; from Indian false vampire bats and tokay geckoes in the kitchen to tarantulas in the walls outside. Jon McGowen used some fishing line and a live cricket to go tarantula fishing, baiting the spider out far enough to be photographed.

The caves themselves were amazing. Apparently they go on for miles with many smaller passages branching off the main cave. Fulvous fruit bats (*Rousettus leschenaulti*) roosted in the cave, and bizarre white fungus sprouted up from their droppings. The waters that ran through the cave were alive with tiny fish, shrimp, crab and cave crayfish. A swarm of them were feeding on a dead bat. Jon found two recently dead bats and decided to take them back with him to be stuffed. Huntsman spiders as broad as a human hand scurried over the rocks. I was excavating in the earth of the cave in the hope of finding some bone material. Pintu, one of the guides/porters found a section of what looked like leg bone under some rocks. It was around six inches long. Upon examining it in the daylight, Jon thought it looked like the femur of a biped. We kept it for later analysis.

The following day we set out across a huge suspension bridge that spanned the Simsang River and began to trek into the jungle. As we entered the forest a huge Bengal eagle owl went crashing through the canopy. As the path rose we glimpsed wild jungle fowl, ancestors of the domestic chicken. This place really did remind me of Kipling's India. We came across an area of limestone outcroppings in the jungle. Some had been sculpted by wind and water to resemble human faces; others looked like the walls of lost temples or ruined cities, though all were natural in formation. This brought to mind the 'Cold Lairs' where the 'Bandar-Log' or monkey people brought Mowgli in 'The Jungle Books' wonderful collections of dark tales so crassly bastardized by Disney. One area in particular was a narrow passage between two limestone cliffs. Rudy and Rufus told us that up until around 20 years ago the passage was used by hunting tigers to ambush men. Humans were forced to walk single file and the walls were too steep and slippery to climb, making the men easy prey for the great cats. Later we came upon a watering hole and searched the mud for tracks; we found elephant, sambur, barking deer and buffalo. At one point as we were resting in the jungle something leapt down from the trees just over a ridge above us. The guides thought it may have been a leopard that was stalking us, but on examination they said it was more likely to have been a monkey. Though we saw none we did find many monkey droppings.

The paradox of the jungle is although it contains the greatest concentration of life anywhere on Earth, animals are more difficult to see here than anywhere else. Creatures can hear a human coming from a long way off and melt like ghosts into the shadows. Wildlife is much easier to spot in open grassland areas. In all my time in many rainforests around the world I've only seen a handful of large animals.

Whilst most of us had been away in the jungle, Dave Archer had stayed by the Simsang searching for snakes and looking for animal tracks. He found the footprints of a tigress in the sand. It was good to know that there were still tigers in the area.

Later we interviewed the head man of the village, Gentar. He had encountered something strange in Siju caves several years before, something that frightened him so much he refused to go back there. He and some friends had been fishing by the light of burning torches. They heard a noise he described as sounding like someone treading on bamboo. On investigation they found wet footprints on the rocks. They were human-like but of a vast size. They led down one of the passages that turned off the main one. The group thought a mande-burung had entered the cave from one of its many jungle entrances.

They panicked and fled the cave.

I found it odd that such a creature would be lurking so close to human habitation, but I was to hear subsequent stories of them approaching other villages. Cave systems retain a stable temperature, it could be the creature entered the caves to keep cool or possibly hunt for crabs.

From Siju we moved down to Bagimara and set up HQ in a delightful lodge with a magnificent view of the Simsang. In the evening we would watch the sun setting over the river from the veranda. I enjoyed several chapters of Kipling's immortal Jungle Books, so cheapened by the infantile Disney films. Of all the places we stopped in India this was my favorite.

Whilst here we were introduced to a local man called Beka. A sculptor by trade, he had an interest in cryptozoology and told us of a story his father related to him. Around 1940 in a lake near the borders of Bangladesh a group of armed men, possibly soldiers, had shot a sankuni. Apparently the creature had devoured a number of people over the years. The creature's body lay partly out of the lake and partly in. The portion out of the lake was said to measure 60 feet. If there was any truth to the story it made me wonder just what kind of firearms would be needed to do any kind of serious damage to a snake so huge, and what happened to the body? The story might be nothing more than a tall tale, but it highlights the belief of a giant crested serpent in the Garos.

More recently, within the last five years, there had been a case of a woman who dreamed a man had warned her that her house was going to be destroyed due to an impending landslide. She moved out of her house that was indeed destroyed by a landslide. Witnesses saw a huge sankuni crawling away from the wreckage. It could be, that if the sankuni is a real, flesh and blood animal, it inhabits underground burrows and lairs. If these are disturbed by a landslide and the animal is seen crawling away, then people may have thought the sankuni's coils had been the cause of the landslide.

We travelled to the village of Imangri and interviewed the head man Shireng R Marak, a 56 year old with two thumbs on his right hand. In 1978 he and some friends were hunting in the forest. As it was beginning to grow dark he heard something big and powerful crashing through the forest. He hear a loud, deep call, AUHH!-AUHH-AUHH!

Which he imitated for us loudly. He had heard village elders talking about the mande-burung and demonstrating the sound it made. He and his friends ran into a cave and lit a fire at the entrance. They heard the creature bellowing and crashing around outside the cave all night. At first light it moved away into the forest and they ran back to the village.

Shireng said sightings of the creature were more common 40 years ago. His friend's grandfather had shot one. He said it was man-like, covered in black fur with a face like a monkey.

The village shaman had supposedly seen the mande-burung as well. Neka Marak was 77 and suffering from cataracts. He made medicines and charms. Back before the Indian / Pakistan war of 1965 he had been searching for an incense tree in the jungle. He came upon some thick creepers that had been snapped by something with immense strength. He heard a crashing sound and turned around to see a huge mande-burung charging at him through the jungle. Neka pointed to the roof of a nearby tea house in the village, in order to give us an idea of the size of the creature. The roof of the tea house was 15 feet high, a size I was totally unable to accept for the mande-burung. I don't know if it was the old man's cataracts making him over estimate, the length of time since the sighting or sheer fear. He went on to say it resembled a huge, hair-covered man. The face looked very human and the hands were big enough to have broken a human's neck. After all this time he could not recall the colour of the creature's fur. To his credit he did not try to embellish, but admitted he could not recall the colour of the hair. He fled from the forest as quickly as he could.

Neka had also seen the sankuni prior to 1965. He saw the creature emerge from a cave beside the Simsang River. He did not see the whole animal as he beat a hasty retreat. He indicated the portion he saw was in the region of 25-30 feet long. It was black scaled with a yellowish underbelly. It had a red, rooster-like crest and red wattles under the lower jaw. He fled in terror from the giant snake.

The following day we drove to Balpakram, an area that looms high in Garo legend. It was thought to be the place the souls of the dead rested before going into the next world. It is a national park and the forested areas are full of wildlife.

The roads grew more treacherous as we drove higher. Soon even the four-wheel drives were struggling to cope. We walked the final couple of miles on foot to the great plateau that formed Balpakram. I noticed the area was heavily used for grazing and there were quite a few people around. Herdsmen were burning off dry grass to promote new growth for grazing their livestock. I found it hard to visualize a large ape or indeed any big animal existing in the area. The basalt rocks in the park were formed into six-sided, geometric forms much like those in the Giant's Causeway in Ireland. The molten rock formed the shapes as it cooled and contracted. Unlike Ireland, there are no columns and the shapes are visible only at ground level. Local people call the strange configuration the 'ghost market.' Rudy told us fossilized pumpkin, melon and tomato seeds have been found in the area, leading to the legend that it is a place where spirits hold a market place at night.

As we walked further across the plateau we finally came across a truly spectacular gorge. Seven kilometers wide, two kilometers across and around one kilometer deep, the Balpakram gorge made an astounding spectacle. It was heavily forested and had near-sheer sides. A river ran through the bottom, and Rudy explained the only safe way in was via canoe by the river from a nearby village. Only two or so hunters ventured into the gorge per year and it was mostly unexplored. It looked as if it could easily hide a small group of yeti in its deep, inaccessible forests. Unfortunately we did not have enough time to investigate the gorge, as such an undertaking would have taken a whole week. We made plans to return to the gorge on a future expedition.

Back at the lodge we met the owner, Bullbully Marak, who told us how keen she was to promote ecotourism in the area. The Garo Hills and Meghalaya in general are not often visited by tourists. Rudy and Rufus mentioned that they often feel like foreigners in their own country, and are often mistaken for Indonesians or Malayans. The feeling throughout the Garos is the Central Government of India is ignoring them. Such feelings have lead to the formation of several insurgent groups in the area.

We returned to the somewhat depressing surroundings of Tura and met up with Dipu once more. We were to spend the next day interviewing a number of people around Tura. The first on our list was Dr Milton Sasama, Pro-Vice-chancellor of Garo Hills University. He had written a number of books on the history and folklore of the Garo Hills. He did not believe in the mande-burung, as he had never come across descriptions of the beast in any of his studies. He had only heard of the monster, like a giant orangutan, in the past 20 years. He also asserted there was no tradition of a yeti-like creature in Assam, the Indian state between the Garo Hills and the Himalayas.

Conversely, he believed implicitly in the sankuni. He knew a man who had eaten the flesh of a dead, juvenile sankuni after it had been washed into a village by a flood. It was between 12 and 20 feet long and bore a rooster-like crest. The meat from the carcass had provided enough food for the whole village. The man, now in his 80s, called Albin Stone, resided in Tura.

Our next interviewee was with Llewellyn Marak, the uncle of Rufus, who was a noted naturalist and author of a number of books on the wildlife of the Garo Hills. In 1999 he came across a set of four, huge, man-like footprints at Nokrek Peak, around 21 km from Tura. They were found in sand beside a stream and were 18 inches long. The tracks lead away into the jungle.

Llewellyn's grandfather was a renowned hunter who amassed a large collection of trophies. He encountered the mande-burung on a hunting trip many years before. He said he came across the beast in a jungle clearing. It resembled a huge gorilla and was black in colour. It moved around on all fours and seemed to be searching for food. Occasionally it would stop and sit, appearing to eat something. Llewellyn's grandfather became afraid and backed away.

This is the only report we have of the creature moving on all fours. Then again it may have been doing this in order to forage for food. The experienced hunter was sure what he had seen was not a bear.

Llewellyn also heard stories of giant catfish and giant freshwater stingrays, much like those said to lurk in the Mekong River of Indo-China.

Following this we moved on to speak to Rufus' uncle, a surgeon called Dr. Lao, who also believed the mande-burung existed, but thought it was now very rare. Dr. Lao had a collection of books on Indian wildlife, among them a book entitled "*A Naturalist in Karbi Anglong*" by Awaruddin Choudry, first published in 1993. The book, by one of India's best known naturalists, records his time in the Karbi Anglong district of Assam, the Indian state to the north of Meghalaya.

One chapter of Chourdy's book is given over to the *khenglong-po*, a yeti-like creature seen in the area. As Assam borders onto Bhutan, there is a link - or corridor if you will - directly from the Himalayas, down to the Garo Hills, along which yetis are reported, and totally refutes Dr. Milton Sasama's assertion that no such creatures are reported from Assam. He writes ...

"Singhason peak and some nearby areas are sacred to the Karbis. Here in the dense forest lives the Khenglong-po, the legendary 'hairy wild-man'. The Khenglong-po is an important figure in the Karbi folk tale. Whenever I used to get reports of its existence, I dismissed them as fable or mistaken identification of an ordinary animal. But when the much experienced Sarsing Rongphar gave me a fresh report, I had to rethink. Sarsing had been my guide in parts of the Dhansiri Reserved Forest, and I found him to be an accurate and reliable observer."

Sarsing Rongphar was Choudry's guide. He was a hunter who used dogs to sniff out game, such as muntjac and porcupine, which he then dispatched with a long hunting knife. Even before his arrival a Karbi along Awaruddin Choudry had heard of sightings of a large, bi-pedal ape. At first he asked witnesses if they might be mistaking a stump tailed macaque (*Macaca arctoides*) or a hoolock gibbon (*Hoolock hoolock*) but the witnesses rejected this, as they were familiar with both species. When his trusted guide told him of an encounter with the beast, Choudry was forced to change his mind.

It was on May 13th 1992 that Sarsing Rongphar, his friend Buraso Terang and his hunting dogs ventured into Dhansiri Reserved Forest. In the afternoon they came upon large man-like footprints around 18 inches long and 6-7 inches wide. The pair followed the tracks for 3 kilometers until their usually brave dogs began to panic. Fearing an elephant or tiger was close by, they crept cautiously forward. Soon a loud breathing sound became audible as a 'khhr-khhhr' sound. From 80-90 meters away they saw an ape-like creature leaning against a tree, apparently asleep. The witnesses were at a higher elevation than the creature and had a clear view, due to the fact there was no dense undergrowth obscuring their view. The creature was jet black like a male hoolock gibbon, with thick bear-like hair on the body. The hair on the head was long and curly. The creature was a female with visible breasts. Its mouth was open, and large, human-like teeth apparent. The face, hands and feet were black and ape-like. In front of the creature was a broken tree, and the hunters thought the creature had been feeding on it. They observed the sleeping animal for around one hour. Sarsing likened it to a giant hoolock gibbon, but with much shorter forearms.

On reaching their village they told tribal elders of what they had seen and were informed it was a Khenglong-po, a kind of hairy Wildman thought to be dangerous.

Choudry took Sarsing to his camp and showed him pictures of the Asian black bear (*Ursus thibetanus*) standing on its hind legs, and the mountain gorilla (*Gorilla beringei beringei*). The hunter identified the latter creatures as being a Khenglong-po whilst recognizing the former for exactly what it was. Choudry interviewed Buraso Terang separately and got the same answers. A Khenglong-po was also once supposed to have wandered up the railway track from Langcholiet to Nailalung.

On another occasion Choudry talked to some hunters from Karbi Anglong in central Assam. They spoke of a large, herbivorous, ground dwelling ape they called *Gammi*. According to them, two Gammis were seen together in 1982, feeding on reeds on the eastern slope of the Karbi Plateau in the upper Deopani area. An elderly hunter encountered one in the Intanki Reserved Forest in Nagaland in 1977-78. The creatures are said to be covered in grey hair and to be man-like in appearance. The name Gammi means 'wild-man'.

We can see then an unbroken link of yeti sightings from Bhutan down into India.

The following day we interviewed another witness. He was a 51 year old teacher called Kingston. In 1987 he and a friend were on Tura peak. He saw large, five-toed, man-like tracks in wet sand beside a stream. The toes and heel extended far beyond his own. My size nines were bigger than Kingston's, and he told me the creature's tracks were bigger than my feet. The tracks sunk an inch into the sand, whereas Kingston's own tracks only sunk in half an inch. He heard the mande-burung's cry, AUHH!-AUHH-AUHH! He imitated the sound, which was in line with that made by other witnesses. He wanted to investigate further but his friend was too afraid. He said he has heard the cry on Tura peak again, within the last few years.

Later that day we visited the village of Apertee, some 35 miles from Tura to meet a witness called Nicholas Sama. In the 1960s he had seen the severed hand and forearm of a mande-burung at a village market. The forearm, which was being displayed on a store selling bushmeat, was as long as his whole arm. The hand looked like a mans but far larger, with long fingernails and the arm covered in long, black hair. Nicholas thought it was very old as the skin was desiccated. No one knew where it had originally come from. Nicholas knew that what he was looking at was not the arm of a bear or a gibbon.

The next day we met with a most impressive witness in the village of Ronbakgre. Teng Sangma had heard that in April of 2004 a village carpenter had seen a female mande-burung suckling an infant in a bamboo forest close to Rongarre. He did not believe the story, but on the 24th of that month he and a friend were hunting jungle fowl in the forest and came across a huge figure sitting with its back to them. Even in its sitting position it was five feet tall. It was covered with dark hair, and had longer hair on its head that fell down onto the shoulders and the back. The shoulders were very broad. It was a female and was suckling a youngster whose legs were visible at the side of its mother, suggesting the infant was sitting on her lap. The youngster was making gurgling noises. The adult was pulling down large bamboo stems and plucking off the leaves to eat. The men got to within 50 feet of the creatures, watched them for 2 minutes before they became afraid, then backed away, leaving the creatures behind. Apparently the creatures had not noticed them.

The following day we met another impressive witness. Nelbison Sangma was a farmer from the village of Sansasico. He observed a mande-burung for three days in 2003. He was some 500 meters from the creature looking down upon it. The creature was on the top of a smaller hill. When he first saw it the mande-burung was standing under a tree. It was nine feet tall and covered with black hair. It moved around for an hour as he watched it. It then slept in a nest apparently constructed by pulling down branches much like a gorilla does. The next day the creature was in the same place and appeared to be sunning itself. This time he watched it for half an hour. On the third day he saw it again, wandering about and foraging.

He later took some other villagers to the area and showed them the nest. There was a monkey-like smell pervading the surroundings. They found man-like tracks 18 inches long and a huge dropping the length of a human forearm. This contained fibers from banana leaves.

We then switched our attention back to Nokrek National Park. On the way we picked up some provisions; namely rice, fruit and several live chickens. These I named Little Lofty, Gloria and Mr Ladidah Gunner Graham, after characters from 'It Ain't Half Hot Mum.' Dave brought a pot of the rice wine we had tried at the Wangala Festival from a roadside vendor.

We stayed in a specially made tourist lodge near a village in the park. It was made to look like a traditional Garo house constructed of wood and bamboo. During the day's exploration we came across a huge man-like track imprinted deep into the sand beside a stream. The print was like a human track but with a couple of important differences. The heel was proportionally broader, indicating a weight-bearing heel. The toes were more even, showing much less of a curve from the big toe down to the little toe. The track was sunk over an inch into the wet sand, whereas my own footprints could not reach even half that depth. We photographed the print with frames of reference.

Back at the lodge we ate dinner then sat around the fire telling stories. I tried some of the rice wine Dave had brought. I was to regret it later. During the night I had severe stomach pains as if someone were twisting a knife in my guts. I felt bloated and feverish. During one of my many visits to the toilet during the night, I heard something large moving around in the darkness outside the lodge. I assumed it was a goat or a cow that had wandered down from the village.

In the morning Rudy told us that something had been pushing against the lodge door. He thought it was a tiger attracted by the live chickens we were keeping inside the lodge. I was feeling worse than ever and was in a lot of pain. I forced myself to go with the others into the jungle on the off chance the creature would put in an appearance. I found the trek hard with my intense stomach pain and fever. At a waterhole I had to stop and rest as the others went on. Dave and Jon found another set of mande-burung tracks by a stream further into the jungle. They followed the stream and seemed fairly fresh. The creature seemed to be overturning rocks and hunting for freshwater crabs. Several crabs were discovered with their insides sucked out. I managed to stagger back to the camp. Thankfully by morning I was feeling better.

We returned to Tura and chased up some leads and loose ends. We photocopied the relevant chapter from Dr Lao's book, then visited the rather shabby library to see if there was anything on the mande-burung and the sankuni. We turned up absolutely nothing. We tried to track down Albin Stone, the man who was said to have eaten the flesh of a dead, juvenile sankuni but he was not at home.

Diup showed us a rib bone found by his father at Balpakram in 1989. I thought it looked more bovid than primate but we took a sample from it. Dipu also showed us a collection of hairs he found at Nokrek in 2006. They looked to me like goral (*Naemorhedus goral*) a goat-like antelope known to inhabit the area. All of these, together with the bone from Siju Caves would be sent to Lars Thomas and his team at Copenhagen University for analysis.

All too soon our time in the Garos was over. We had to say our goodbyes to Dipu, Rudy, Rufus and the others. We returned to Delhi and then back to England.

As I suspected the hair turned out to be goral and the bone bovid. The leg bone from the cave, however, was human.

I am convinced the mande-burung exists and that it is one in the same as the larger kind of yeti. The best model we have for this animal is a surviving form of *Gigantopethicus blacki*, a giant ape known from fossil teeth and jaw bones found in India, China and Vietnam. The jaw structure seems to indicate *Gigantopethicus* was a biped. It lived as recently as 500,000 years ago, the blink of an eye in evolutionary terms, and it seems likely that it may still inhabit the wilder parts of Asia. As for the sankuni, its startling resemblance to the Indo-Chinese naga, the West African ninki-nanka, the Central African crested crowing cobra and many other monster serpents, convinces me there are more to these stories than hot air.

There is talk of the CFZ returning to the Garos in a few years time, probably to mount an expedition down into the rarely visited gorge at Balpakram. Kipling's India is still alive if you look hard enough, and I intend to return there.

Wood Knocks | Journal of Sasquatch Research, Volume II

Interdimensional Paraphysical Sasquatch
by Rosemary Ellen Guiley

[Author's note: The Sasquatch have conveyed to people that they do not appreciate the term "Bigfoot," which they consider demeaning. Native American names for them are preferable. Consequently, I have refrained from using "Bigfoot," except in cases where I am quoting someone verbatim. I am sympathetic and in agreement with this preference, as the Sasquatch are not "animals," "creatures," or "monsters," but intelligent beings. I have chosen to use "Sasquatch" as a default, as this name, from the Coast Salish of the Pacific Northwest, is widely recognized.

I would like to express my thanks to Joe Burcaw, who gave permission for his full story to be told for the first time in print.]

Encountering Sasquatch was not on Joe Burcaw's radar the day he went hiking in one of his favorite areas in the Litchfield Hills in southwestern Connecticut. In fact, he had no interest in looking for Sasquatch. That day in 2012 changed everything.

It was late October, the day after hurricane Sandy battered Connecticut. Burcaw, who lived in New York City, took a run up to Litchfield County to check on his family members living there. Curious to see the storm damage from the high winds and rain to his favorite haunts in the hills, he decided to go out for a hike.

Burcaw grew up near the Litchfield Hills, and had been hiking, mountain biking and cross country skiing in the area since the 1980s. He was intimately familiar with the terrain.

He arrived at one of his favorite spots in the mid- to late afternoon.

His destination was an old abandoned mining tunnel deep in the woods. The storm devastation he found was difficult to absorb. Huge, majestic cedar trees were toppled over like toothpicks snapped in half, and flooding from a river spread all over the walking trails.

The damage hindered his progress, and it took him longer than usual to reach the old mining tunnel. The woods here always felt strange and eerie—one of the attractions for him. The place had never been very active with wildlife and had always given off a sense something invisible was watching. Burcaw experienced times when the birds and insects went from vibrant to complete silence for hours.

Today the environment felt stranger than usual. There was absolute silence, and it was uncanny, almost unsettling.

For some reason, Burcaw kept feeling the urge to look down. He did so, and noticed the multitude of leaves covering the muddy path leading into the tunnel. Something caught his attention. Curious, he wiped away leaves, and uncovered what looked like a foot print—but this was no ordinary footprint.

His first thought was that it was not a human boot print from someone who got out there investigating before him. He took a closer look, and then knew without a doubt the print was not human-made at all. It was much larger than his size 11 shoe, maybe a size 15. Even stranger, there were no other prints near it, just the single footprint, as though dropped from space.

Burcaw fished out his flip phone camera and snapped a few shots so he could blow them up for a more detailed look when he got home. Seconds after he finished taking the photos, wood knocking sounded somewhere out in the distance, and a "god awful" screeching echoed throughout the entire valley. It sounded like a dog or some sort of animal in distress. Another 20 seconds later, a large tree fell over on the side of the valley opposite the screeching.

Alarmed, and not sure what was happening, Burcaw decided to get the hell out. He put his camera away and headed at a quick pace back to where he had parked his car, some distance away. He was acutely aware that suddenly dusk was closing in, and the sky was darkening rapidly. He picked up his pace, blood pumping.

The screeching continued along with the wood knocking, but subsided as he drew close to his vehicle. He flung open the door and slid inside, flooded with relief and the odd thought he was lucky to have gotten there in one piece. Never before, in all the years he had spent time alone and with friends in these woods, had he encountered something so mysterious and frightening.

On that day, a door to an alternate reality opened for Joe Burcaw, never to close. Sasquatch had introduced itself, and it had a purpose.

Up until then, Burcaw believed in the existence of Sasquatch, even though he had no compunction to search them out. They deserved human respect and to be left alone, in his view. Now he was on their radar. From then on for years, wood knocks greeted him whenever he entered the forest by himself.

In early November 2012, less than a week after his initial encounter with an unseen Sasquatch, a light snow fell, leaving behind a few inches on the ground. Burcaw was still visiting his family, and decided to go back up to the woods. This time, he was fully prepared with cameras and video units. It was a reasonable idea to try to capture evidence. As he would soon learn, however, Sasquatch do not appreciate attempts at photography. They make themselves known on their own terms, not on human terms.

Burcaw arrived at the trail and made it halfway to the old mining tunnel, when he saw different tracks in the snow which he recognized as human. The tracks were single and had no pairing whatsoever. He knew what bear and cougar tracks looked like, and these were not made by those animals. Some of the tracks looked bipedal, with large talons sticking out of the toes. Other tracks defied identification.

Burcaw pulled out his camera and took some pictures. Immediately, he was overcome by a rush of dread and a pounding headache, as though something or someone was shooting fear into his body. A thought rose in his mind that he was trespassing, and some species of Sasquatch was sending the message that it wanted him to get out of the spot. He wasted no time jamming his belongings in his pack, then jogged back to his car.

There was no apparent pursuit—at least in physical terms. What happened next ramped up the high strangeness index in Burcaw's life.

A few nights later, he had a vision or astral projection in the early morning hours while sleeping. It was one of those intense, lucid dream-like experiences, in which a person feels awake and the experience is "real," not a dream.

"I was completely coherent and present," said Burcaw. "It was almost as though I was in complete control, yet someone else was invading my personal space, causing me to feel violated and out of control. It's hard to put into words, but it wasn't a comforting situation by any means."

An out of the ordinary scenario unfolded right before him. Burcaw found himself back in his childhood neighborhood of Litchfield County, Connecticut. He was not in his own home, but in the home of a childhood friend, and he was staring out his friend's bedroom window. An Asian woman who looked to be in her late fifties was running frantically, as though for her life, across the front lawn. Two disc-shaped craft came into view and hovered, switching from a horizontal position to a vertical position. The craft then landed behind trees across the street, close to where the woman was fleeing. Then two black SUVs pulled up close to the house, and two men stepped out of the trucks. They carried weapons that looked like old-fashioned sub machine guns beneath their long trench coats. The guns reminded Burcaw of those from the gangster era in the early twentieth century.

The men—who Burcaw felt were Men in Black, wore white surgical masks on their faces, obscuring their features. He could see, however, that their skin was not human-looking, but had a blue tint. One MIB wore a beige trench coat and the other wore a black one. They were obviously in hot pursuit of the Asian woman—they meant business.

Burcaw, still in this alternate reality, started to feel panicky and felt the urge to throw himself under a bed for cover. There was one near him in the bedroom. Just as he slid under the bed, he heard footsteps enter the room and saw two sets of legs standing directly in front of him. His adrenaline was pumping as he wondered frantically what he should do.

The two MIB spoke to each other about the woman, and where they should search next for her. She evidently possessed information they did not want disclosed to the public. Burcaw prayed they would not look under the bed. They did not seem to be in pursuit of him, but he was certain they were aware of his existence.

Then the weird experience ended.

After he awoke, Burcaw puzzled over it. It seemed dream-like, but it was a "100 percent real" experience, and he was in complete control of his actions. He soon contacted author and investigator Nick Redfern, who told him he had heard of similar experiences from others.

There was much more to come. There were no more MIB visits, but black helicopters occasionally buzzed his home. In 2015 Burcaw moved back to Connecticut, not far from where he grew up, and the helicopters continued to show up. There was no pattern to them, but as of this writing their frequency was declining.

I asked Burcaw for his interpretation of the MIB "dream" experience. Was it a warning?

"The MIB experience was a scare tactic of what could happen to me if I pursued investigating Sasquatch," he said. "Our government/ secret government have a boatload of information about Sasquatch that they want kept quiet from the general public."

He said he protected himself from the MIB with white light and a high spiritual energy. "The MIB have no consciousness and cannot function if confronted with the Christ figure or angelic realm," Burcaw said. "They see that world as a threat and therefore back off if someone is strong enough to deflect their harassment. I told them to f— off and to never contact me again. I possess a stronger constitution than they thought, because I know who they are, and what they do to people with their bullshit intimidation tactics. I haven't seen or heard from them since. The black helicopters buzzing my condo have diminished, too, at least for the time being."

With the intimidation halted in the early stages, other paranormal activity with Sasquatch increased. Burcaw began having more encounters with them went he went into the woods alone. As these encounters increased, the incidences of wood knocking decreased. A new type of apparent surveillance began: hovering white planes when he went into the woods.

The Sasquatch are "in the astral world," Burcaw said. "I have seen 95 percent of my sightings of Sasquatch through the dream state, yet I have complete control of my body and actions while having the experience," he said. "My first sighting was of a large male hiding behind a robust oak tree, sticking its head out and peeking at me from

10-20 yards away. I was on a path leading out to a field where this single tree was located. This was an observation scenario, some sort of test to see how I would react." The field reminded him of a field behind a house in his childhood neighborhood.

On another occasion, he witnessed a "youngling" accidentally falling out of a tree. "The youngling, who I caught out of the corner of my eye, was completely embarrassed," he said. "Initially, I heard a loud tree branch snap, and then had the image of it falling to the ground with a thump. I saw a dark figure for a brief second before it phased out and disappeared. My feeling was that the youngling broke a rule by getting too close to me—a human—and had to get back home before he was reprimanded by his elders."

Sometimes the Sasquatch would phase in and out like the ripply presence of Predator in the film of the same title.

Evidently, Burcaw passed the tests with the Sasquatch, for in mid-2016, his encounters took a new and dramatic turn, involving visits to space craft and being in the presence of Sasquatch and aliens.

"I made communication with a male clan leader named Girdock, who asked for my help in healing his wounded father," Burcaw said. "I was aboard a space craft with Girdock, his life partner and son. There were high-ranking humanoid Pleiadians with us, too, assisting in the healing. The four-foot greys were operating on the wounded Sasquatch. They wore surgical attire that was all in white, and they used rod-like devices to heal the wounds. I could sense from their thoughts that they needed universal loving consciousness for this operation to be a success. The elder leader did make it out alive and was very loving and appreciative of our help. He had white hair and reminded me of the abominable snow man. He was very weak from his surgery and wounds and needed to rest."

Burcaw said until the space craft experience, his Sasquatch encounters had been solely with males. The female life partner of Girdock was the first encounter he had with a female.

"I asked Girdock why I haven't seen them in the past, and he explained that they're highly protective of the female population from the outside human world," Burcaw said. "You have to earn their trust as an outsider to have contact with the women, which is almost never. They're attracted to higher consciousness, and I have displayed this since I was a child."

This brings in another facet of meaningful contact with Sasquatch shared by many experiencers: a history of otherworldly experiences and contact from an early age. Some individuals have an inborn, heightened capability of attracting and interacting with beings and spirits. From childhood, they experience ghosts, visitations from the dead, spirit contact, UFO sightings, anomalous creature sightings and more. I have seen this across the board in my research in the paranormal, cryptids, ufology and metaphysics fields. Not everyone who has a contact experience shares this life-history trait, but a significant number do. Burcaw is in this category: a frequent experiencer of the paranormal and extraordinary from a young age.

Such individuals are described as having an "encounter-prone personality," a term put forward by Dr. Kenneth Ring, a leading near-death experience (NDE) researcher, in his book *The Omega Project*, 1990 and 1992. Encounter-prone individuals dissociate more easily than others, and once they have unusual experiences, are more open to having them in the future. Encounter-prone individuals also tend to have heightened intuitive/psychic and artistic abilities. Thus, they may be more open to intrusions of alternate realities, which, for them, are natural extensions of this reality.

Many experiencers feel they are chosen for contact. Do other beings and spirits take note of certain individuals, watch them, and then contact them? Burcaw is certain of that concerning the Sasquatch: They watched over him for years without him knowing it. Around 2012, he underwent a significant shift in spiritual development—and contact was initiated on that trip into the woods after Sandy.

"They have contacted me for a reason, why I am not sure," said Burcaw. "On separate occasions, I have left them fruits and cakes as a token of my appreciation, and was left in return (days later) a single quartz crystal off the side of a trail, sitting on a log. I have always felt a close connection to the Sasquatch and hope someday to be able to converse with them on a consistent basis. I am not afraid but curious, and hope my encounters will lead me toward more hidden discoveries. I have yet to see them face to face in this realm, but hope that will change with time."

Paraphysical Characteristics

Burcaw has plenty of company. While most reported Sasquatch "events" are fleeting sightings and contacts, there are an increasing number of people coming forward with accounts of paraphysical characteristics, and intelligent and meaningful interaction with sophisticated beings.

Paraphysical and paranormal characteristics of Sasquatch encounters also are widely reported in sightings and encounters with dogmen, mystery cats, assorted other cryptids, aliens and extraterrestrials, Black-Eyed People, Men and Women in Black, faeries and even the Djinn—in short, other beings and entities that humans have encountered throughout the ages in a variety of forms. The most commonly reported experiences are:

- Telepathic communication.
- Sudden, unexplained appearance (possible materialization).
- Sudden, unexplained disappearance into thin air or into solid matter (possible dematerialization).
- Disappearance in flashes of light.
- Rapid movement, including instant relocation (possible teleportation).
- Isolated footprints, sometimes single, that suddenly end.
- Observed walking in snow, but leaves no footprints.
- Appears to float or glide rather than walk.
- Invisibility or cloaking.
- Shape-shifting, as though the form is not definite or "completely in" our dimension.
- Appears to be impervious to bullets (although some have communicated that they know bullets can kill).
- Deliberate eye contact that conveys intelligence and telepathic messages.

And in some cases:

- Feelings of being constantly watched or tracked after an initial encounter.
- Additional encounters, as though the person has been "tagged."
- Subsequent paranormal activity in the home, and/or bedroom experiences.
- Synchronistic UFO sightings and activity, or other cryptid or entity encounters.

These characteristics do not occur in all cases, perhaps not even in a majority—but they occur with enough frequency to indicate something other than encounters with "normal" animals or species is afoot. Yet some cryptid investigators resolutely cling to their convictions that Sasquatch and other strange entities are nothing more than "lost" or "hidden" physical Earth species, despite that encounters with lions, bears, birds, and other denizens of wild Earth are not accompanied by a raft of high strangeness.

Paul G. Johnson, a Pennsylvania researcher, observes, "There is no doubt that the Pennsylvania Bigfoot is real. ... The problem is that our Bigfoot simply does not possess the same properties as the other indigenous Pennsylvania animals." [1]

Nick Redfern, who has done extensive research on cryptids and UFOs, as well as related phenomena, notes, "Theorists suggest the reason why we lack a body of Bigfoot—and the reason for their near-mystifying, overwhelming elusiveness—is because the creatures are the denizens of a vast underworld; animals that spend most of their time living in dark caves and deep caverns, unknown to man, and which extend and spread for miles underground." [2]

There may be a physical component to the dwelling places of Sasquatch, or at least preferred locales when they are present in this reality. Trying to fit all the reported paraphysical phenomena into a physical explanation is impossible, however.

There is no one-size-fits-all explanation. There seem to be varieties of Sasquatch, just as there are marked differences among human beings. They do not all exhibit the same behavior. Some are wary, curious, or hostile, and some have reached out in benevolent telepathic communication. Some have exhibited sexual interest in humans. As intelligent beings, they do not all have the same motives or interests. Humans certainly do not.

It is difficult to gauge the true incidence of paraphysical Sasquatch contacts, as well as intelligent interaction. Experiencers still fear ridicule, and so remain silent. And, biased researchers, including organizations, disregard or discredit reports pointing to an intelligent, interdimensional being with telepathic power and connections to UFO activity. [3] Other researchers, looking for "politically correct" ground to stand on, offer such reports and data but take an "I don't know what's going on" position. Linda S. Godfrey is one of the exceptions among researchers, delving into the paraphysical realm in *"Monsters Among Us: An Exploration of Otherworldly Bigfoots, Wolfmen, Portals, Phantoms, and Odd Phenomena"* (2016), which focuses on dogmen and Sasquatch experiences.

Native Americans, on the other hand, (as discussed later in this article) have had no discomfort accepting the existence of interdimensional, paraphysical Sasquatch.

Can science explain?

Does science have an explanation for beings such as Sasquatch, their unusual characteristics and our experiences with them? There are two that address aspects of Sasquatch encounters, but neither offers "official" scientific proof of the existence of the beings. However, they do point in the direction of the paraphysical and interdimensional.

In physics, M Theory, also known as "many worlds," posits there are dimensions, or "branes," stacked together in our universe, each vibrating at different frequencies. Most of the time, they are invisible to one another. There is interaction between branes, or parallel worlds, under certain conditions, such as leakage or bleed-throughs.

In paranormal research, these leakages seem to occur in openings called "portals." Portals may exist in locations big and small all over the planet. Many are hot spots where all manner of sightings, encounters and paranormal activity are ongoing.

Linda S. Godfrey comments:

"It's been an eye-opening experience for me to learn just how many witnesses of creatures unknown to science have reported weird anomalies either in the creatures themselves or in the vicinity of the sightings. Parareality constructs like portals, fairy paths, UFOs, and even the telepathic, sometimes invisible "alien animals of Janet and Colin Bord" begin to look less fantastic and more like viable pieces of the great puzzle that is our world. The very definition of the word "reality" warps and shimmers as we learn that recent scientific discoveries support the possibility of parallel universes." [4]

The Quantum Hologram Theory (QHT) posits there is an underlying quantum reality that embraces both the physical and the paraphysical—they are flip sides of the same coin. Most encounters take place in a shifted or alternate reality, such as the lucid dream state. Experiencers also describe time standing still or expanding, or being thrust into some sort of "matrix reality" that is Earth but is not. Suddenly everything feels "weird" and there is a cessation of normal noise, including bird, insect and animal life. These conditions persist throughout the encounter or experience, and then just as suddenly, the "normal world" snaps back into place.

The QHT provides a model for non-local consciousness. It holds that the universe is not a three-dimensional spatial construct, but a four-dimensional construct, including time. It is holographic in nature. When a person is in a high state of resonance with the quantum whole, extraordinary events can occur, such as telepathy, out-of-body projection, teleportation and so on.

The UFO connection

A connection exists between Sasquatch sightings and UFO activity: The two sometimes happen in conjunction with each other, or both happen repeatedly in the same areas. This connection does not occur in the majority of Sasquatch reports, but it does happen often enough to raise questions about the meaning of it. For example, researcher Stan Gordon documented many cases of overlapping Sasquatch and UFO activity in Pennsylvania in the 1973-74 wave of activity, as noted in his book *Silent Invasion: The Pennsylvania UFO-Bigfoot Casebook*" (2010). A few years earlier, John Keel documented Sasquatch reports along with UFO activity, encounters with ET's, and other high strangeness that occurred during the Mothman flap in Point Pleasant, West Virginia, in 1966-67.

Other leading researchers have noted the connection, although few explanations have been put forward by either cryptid or UFO investigators. It's a hot potato, and few want to touch it. Understandable, given the interdimensional characteristics of UFO and ET contact: craft and beings that phase in and out of physical reality and move through solid matter; communication via telepathy; supernormal abilities exhibited by alien beings; and experiences that happen in "matrix" realities involving altered states of consciousness.

Contact for transformation

The Edgar Mitchell Foundation for Research into Extraterrestrial Encounters (FREE), of which I am a board director and member of the research committee, has conducted the world's largest survey of experiencers—more than 2,900 persons to date. Results released in February 2016 reveal a host of paranormal and paraphysical phenomena, associated with all kinds of entity and UFO contacts, including Sasquatch-like beings, along with ETs, "energy beings," and others. Sasquatch-like beings comprise about 13 percent of the beings cited by the study experiencers. The bulk are energy beings (unknown life forms with no physicality), short and tall greys and humanoids, followed by reptilians and insectoids. FREE supports the Quantum Hologram Theory as the best explanation for paraphysical and alternate reality contact. [5]

The implications of contact point to marked psycho-spiritual and physical changes in the experiencers that are in line with the kundalini awakenings described in Yoga, which lead to enlightened states of consciousness. In fact, experiencers say the purposes of their contact experiences are the resulting transformations themselves: a greater awareness of the connectedness of all things, and the importance of "love and oneness." That may strike the nuts and bolts and physical evidence adherents as "Spacey New Agey," but the implications are profound, and require a complete reorientation in our approach to research. All our paranormal, spiritual and para-physical experiences are interconnected—"entangled" in the language of quantum physics—and they are wrapped into a bigger picture heavy with spiritual meaning. Not religious. Spiritual.

This is not to say every sighting or encounter with something mysterious is tinged with the spiritual and cosmic. A great deal depends on how the experiencer reacts. A mere sighting can cause a profound change in one individual, yet only seem "weird" or "scary" to another.

Nonetheless, the evidence from experiencers and the results of the FREE study indicate human beings are, on a global scale, having encounters that are changing them physically and at the deepest levels of their being.

This is old news to Kewaunee Lapseritis, the leading advocate of the psychic, ET and paraphysical natures of Sasquatch and their roles in human development. Lapseritis, a holistic health consultant, master herbalist and master dowser, was contacted simultaneously by a Sasquatch and ET in 1979, and got the big picture. Like the experiencers who participated in the FREE study, he developed psychic ability overnight and underwent a spiritual transformation. Since then he has fostered deep relationships with Sasquatch, described in his books *"The Psychic Sasquatch and Their UFO Connection"* (2005) and *"The Sasquatch People and Their Interdimensional Connection"* (2011). He stresses the importance of learning telepathy, and teaches it to individuals who are sincere about having a meaningful contact. The beings respond to those with an open heart and sincerity.

The Native American viewpoint

Many Native Americans regard Sasquatch paraphysical beings—spiritual or interdimensional—who have great psychic powers. Not all Native Americans see Sasquatch as interdimensional—in the Pacific Northwest, he is regarded as a physical creature, albeit an advanced elder brother of humanity. Elsewhere across North America, Sasquatch resides in another world, and enters the world of human beings to teach, protect and warn. Sasquatch is, again, an "elder brother" to people, not an animal, monster, or mysterious creature.

The Sasquatch have superior abilities, such as invisibility, psychic powers, shape-shifting and more. Such beliefs are found among such diverse peoples as the Hopi, Sioux, Iroquois, Northern Athabascan, Athapascan, Lakota and Dakota. The Objibway and Algonquin identify Sasquatch with the Wendigo or Ho-Chunk.

Messengers for change

According to Lapseritis, as well as Native American lore, one of Sasquatch's purposes is as a messenger to humanity, specifically to convey warnings about our destructive ways. They urge humanity to mend its ways or face disaster. Their messages include the need to have more respect for the Earth, to get rid of wicked and evil behavior, to live in peace and harmony and to get back on the spiritual track. From that perspective, they are the spiritual protectors of the land, a concept found universally in mythology. Every people and nation have protectors who appear in times of distress to want and help restore order.

Lapseritis states that Sasquatch have been increasing their appearances worldwide since 2000 with this purpose in mind. They make use of their psychic network to communicate with humans everywhere:

"They want to sensitize the public and validate that they do indeed exist and are a part of our physical world. They have also repeatedly said that if man continues at the rate of destruction of the biosphere, with our dysfunctional and socio-political behavior and blasé attitude toward ecological issues, then all races—including humanity—are doomed. To save the planet is to save ourselves as well as our Sasquatch neighbors… The Sasquatch will help show us the way, if we would only seek out their wisdom from our hearts, not with a gun or just the intellect." [6]

To that end, Kelly Lapseritis, Kewaunee's wife, has been working with DawahOuta LomaKatski (Sunbow TrueBrother, or Sunbow), to publish Sunbow's extensive channeled messages from Kamooh, a Sasquatch Elder Brother, which he began receiving in May 2015. According to Kamooh, both humans and Sasquatch were bioengineered by Star Elders. Sasquatch came first, and then helped humans to adapt to this world.

"We were also gifted with powerful psychic abilities that we have kept to this day including telepathy, mind reading, remote viewing, hypnosis, astral projection, dematerialization, teleportation, shape shifting and permeating consciousness. This last ability allows us to impregnate an area and surround entities with our soul. So we might be perceived as interdimensional beings, but in reality we are an incarnated species with highly developed psychic powers like none other from this home-planet." [7]

The channelings are detailed and extensive about the history of Earth and how Sasquatch have been greatly reduced in numbers due to the actions of humans. In reaching out to select persons, Sasquatch, in concert with the Star Elders, have been providing teachings on interdimensionality through psychic experiences, dreams, astral travels and information downloads.

Lapseritis and other contactees hold that the Sasquatch will continue to avoid the "bag a Bigfoot" hunter types bristling with guns and gear, and instead seek out individuals with a more receptive and refined consciousness. According to Sunbow, Sasquatch do not seek to be photographed or have their DNA identified, because they sense, through remote viewing of humans, how this evidence will be misused and manipulated.

The only approach to study Sasquatch that really seems to bring some genuine results is to see them for who they are: an ancient, highly spiritual, Elder Brother. This means to stop seeing them as animals or primitive hominids that we could trick or trap for curiosity.

But the scientists and Humanity in general will never understand Sasquatch until they think outside of the box and feel existence beyond the limiting [sic] materialist mind frame. Interdimensional beings prove by their existence that there are other planes or dimensional levels of existence where other intelligent life forms dwell. It also reminds us that we too are interdimensional beings, but have forgotten and lost most of our psychic abilities and perceptions, getting trapped in the physical 3D because of materialism. [8]

A model for humanity

The seemingly supernormal abilities of Sasquatch can be mastered by human beings. As mentioned earlier, in Yoga, intense spiritual development and training through meditation and spiritual practices raise the kundalini force, a psycho-spiritual energy that lies dormant in most people. When activated, it energizes the chakra system and expands consciousness. The siddhis are byproducts of this expansion: psychic powers, psychokinetic powers (ability to influence matter), teleportation, bilocation and the ability to make one's self invisible by changing the "vibration" of the body, to cite a few. Sasquatch is ahead of our game, having developed these abilities long before us.

Developing and using these powers wisely requires advanced spiritualized consciousness cultivated through meditation, spiritual discipline and study. Now, however, the FREE study points to an emerging new model: the contact experience as catalyst for change. The mode of contact suits what is appropriate for the individual. For some, it will be ET's, for others, angels and "energy beings," and for others, it will be Sasquatch. Combinations of contact experiences happen as well; there is no requirement that contact take one form only.

In conclusion

Meaningful research and advancement of knowledge about Sasquatch will remain mired if researchers refuse to look beyond the physical for explanations. We should not abandon the search for physical evidence. However, investigators need to get off the dime and stop equivocating and fence-sitting when it comes to the mounting paraphysical evidence. "I don't know" is not an answer and does not serve the field, other researchers and the public. We do not yet know all the answers—but we need to make a start. We need to put ideas, possible explanations and hypotheses on the table, and then follow the data—all the data—into new directions. For those who choose to go bravely into interdimensional explorations, a wealth of discoveries awaits.

The question for researchers is, "Are you old paradigm or are you new paradigm?"

Endnotes

1. Paul G. Johnson, The Bigfoot Phenomenon in Pennsylvania (Privately published, 2007), 75.

2. Nick Redfern, The Bigfoot Book: The Encyclopedia of Sasquatch, Yeti and Cryptid Primates. (Canton, MI: Visible Ink Press, 2016), xv-xvi.

3. Lapseritis, The Sasquatch People and Their Interdimensional Connection, (Comanche Spirit Publishing, 2011), 190.

4. Linda S. Godfrey, Monsters Among Us: An Exploration

of Otherworldly Bigfoots, Wolfmen, Portals, Phantoms, and Odd Phenomena, (New York: Tarcher Perigee, 2016), 342.

5. The complete FREE data, survey, analyses, and papers are posted at www.experiencer.org.

6. Lapseritis, op. cit., 212.

7. SunBow, as told by Sasquatch Elder Brother Kamooh, The Sasquatch Message to Humanity: Conversations with Elder Kamooh, (Comanche Spirit Publishing, 2016), chapter 1.

8. Sunbow, Facebook post, December 7, 2015, (https://www.facebook.com/sasquatchpeople/posts/1029923260361625)

Resources for further reading

Godfrey, Linda. S. Monsters Among Us: An Exploration of Otherworldly Bigfoots, Wolfmen, Portals, Phantoms and Odd Phenomena. New York: Tarcher Perigee, 2016.

Gordon, Stan. Silent Invasion: The Pennsylvania UFO-Bigfoot Casebook. Privately published, 2010.

Johnson, Paul G. The Bigfoot Phenomenon in Pennsylvania. Privately published, 2007.

Keel, John A. The Mothman Prophecies. New York: E.P. Dutton, 1975.

Lapseritis, Kewaunee. The Psychic Sasquatch and Their UFO Connection. CreateSpace, 2005.

_____. The Sasquatch People and Their Interdimensional Connection. Comanche Spirit Publishing, 2011.

Phantoms and Monsters: Pulse of the Paranormal. Daily blog by Lon Strickler. http://www.phantomsandmonsters.com.

Redfern, Nick. The Bigfoot Book: The Encyclopedia of Sasquatch, Yeti and Cryptid Primates. Canton, MI: Visible Ink Press, 2016.

SunBow, as told by Sasquatch Elder Kamooh. The Sasquatch Message to Humanity: Conversations with Elder Kamooh. Comanche Spirit Publishing, 2016.

Wood Knocks | Journal of Sasquatch Research, Volume II

Legendary Encounters with West Virginia Sasquatch
by Dave Spinks

Being born in the Mountains of West Virginia I was raised to be an avid outdoorsman. As young children, most West Virginians are taught how to become self sufficient. We hunt, fish and grow our own gardens, and are considered to be very proficient in the use of firearms. The military has been full of West Virginians sought out for their exceptional shooting and survival skills. I grew up hunting and fishing with my dad, both grandfathers, my uncles and cousins, and relished the time spent in the woods with my family. They don't call West Virginia "Wild and Wonderful" and "Almost Heaven" for nothing.

During Hunting season at "Deer Camp," as we call it here, a typical day would start well before dawn, you'd grab a quick bite to eat, and be in your deer blind or tree stand at least an hour before the sun comes up, in the hopes you wouldn't spook any game within range of your stand. When you were a young buck, you would always be accompanied by an older member of the family in case anything went wrong. I remember how creepy it would be in the woods during that hour or so before daylight, your eyes would sometimes play tricks on you, and you would see things that were downright creepy in nature, often appearing to move silently through the brush and trees. I often couldn't wait to reach my tree stand, because I knew there was only one way up to it, and if anything else would attempt to come up it would be met by the end of the barrel of my rifle, so I felt safe in my tree stand. We would often spend many hours of the day in our stands hoping to get a shot at a monster buck, often seeing an occasional bobcat, fox, bear or squirrel. Then we would come back to camp, eat lunch, maybe take a nap, check our gear and then head back out for the evening hunt.

I enjoyed the evening hunts much better than the morning. During the day the animals seemed to slow down somewhat, compared to what I call the 'magic hour,' just before sunset when the woods seem to come alive with activity; the birds are busy chirping, the squirrels gathering nuts and the deer are done resting for the day, up and moving around getting ready to start feeding for the night. It was eeriest to me after the sun went down. When all the animals would seem to just disappear and go silent. I'd hold my vigil until well after dark, because I was taught not to come out of my stand until it was too dark to see. I could not get down fast enough at times to jump on my ATV and get back to camp. Primarily because I was usually freezing cold and hungry, as well as excited to see and hear the stories of what the others had experienced during their hunt. I looked forward to sitting by the fire and listening to my dad, grandfather's and uncles telling past tales of the hunts they had, as well as occasional stories of strange things they themselves or others they knew had experienced in the vast woods of our home state.

We would often hear stories of strange lights in the sky, occasional mountain lion sightings and strange unnatural screams, howls, whoops and wood knocking sounds coming out of the woods at night. This excited me to no end, wondering what was causing these strange happenings in the woods I spent so much time in. On the flip side, it also sent shivers down my spine thinking about what it might be.

The story that unnerved me the most was one my mother's father told me about the giant hairy men that would hide in the woods and wait to ambush anyone that dared to trespass on their land. My grandfather, 'Papa,' told me that Pete, a good friend of his who he had known many years growing up, shared this story with him when they were both out for a hunt many years ago. He said that Pete and he had been tracking deer all day and had not seen any deer whatsoever, no fresh sign at all, and had walked many miles. I thought this strange, because almost anywhere in the woods of West Virginia you are sure to see a deer or fresh sign of deer, whether it be tracks or scat, pretty much anywhere you look, unless the deer are actually severely spooked by something. Papa said they were hunting in a rugged Hollow in

Braxton county, a place I'm quite familiar with, and I have never been there and NOT seen a deer.

Dave Spinks on the search for Sasquatch

Papa said they were both really tired from walking so many miles trying to find deer so they decided to sit down and take a break and eat. He said "Pete was acting real funny, nervous and twitchy-like, and his eyes were wide as saucers." He asked Pete what the heck was the matter with him, and all Pete would say was "its them damn Wooley Boogers, they are out here, I can feel them watching us."

"Wooley Booger? What the hell is that?" asked my grandfather. Pete then went on to tell a story about how his dad and grandfather were in these very woods many years earlier, they were on their way to town to pick up some supplies at the local hardware store and it was about a 12 mile ride on horseback. They made it to the store, got the supplies and were on their way back home. It was getting dark, and as they approached a very thick patch of woods the horses started acting skittish, and began to buck and kick wildly. They were wary about going into this particular patch of woods. He said it had his dad and grandfather bewildered at why the horses were acting so out of character. Pete's dad said this horrible putrid smell hit them like a ton of bricks. He described it as the worst skunk you ever smelled in your life. They couldn't for the life of them figure out what was causing the smell. Pete said his grandfather then kicked his horse in order to make it move forward into the dense woods. Back in those days there were not many roads other than horse trails and wagon trails through most of West Virginia, they really had no choice but to keep moving. As they moved forward into the woods the horses became more agitated and then they heard the scariest thing they had ever heard in their lives, a loud howling scream that would make your blood run cold. Pete's dad told him he wet his pants, and his grandfather yelled for him to get his horse moving so they could get out of there.

As they got the horses in a good trot, almost a gallop, a giant hairy man jumped out of a tree about 30 yards in front of them. The horses stopped in their tracks and almost bucked them off. Pete went on to describe how his dad said it was very tall, it's chest was dead even with a full grown horses head. Just as they were trying to turn around and get the hell out of there they noticed there was another one off to their right. Pete's Dad told of how it was hollering and throwing large stones at them. He said "I turned my horse to the left and I couldn't believe it — there was another one— and I heard my dad screaming for me to get the hell out of there."

Pete's dad said he kicked his horse as hard as he could trying to flee. He went on to say ,"all I cared about was putting as much space between me and those giant hairy men. I was so scared that I didn't even realize my dad was nowhere in sight. When I realized dad wasn't with me I was petrified, I didn't know if they got him or if he got away and I couldn't bring myself to go back to see if he was ok. I slowed my horse hoping and praying that my dad would catch up to me, all the while my head was on a swivel constantly searching the wood line for any sight of these large, hairy beasts."

He started to cry because he feared those things had got his dad. "I then heard several gun shots in the distance, and I knew it was my dad and he was alive." He was so scared he had forgotten he had a pistol on him, and after he heard the distant shots he gained enough courage to head back towards his dad, firing several rounds in the air to let him know where he was.

"I got about 150 yards from where it happened, and there was just enough light left to see my dad coming at a full gallop and I fired my pistol again so he would know I was there waiting for him." As his father got closer, Pete could see that he was riding funny in the saddle, as if he was hurt. As he got closer Pete's dad said to his father "you ok?" and his father replied "No boy, I'm not. My arms broken." He had a large knot and gash on his head that was bleeding heavily, then added "ride boy, and don't look back."

They ended up going a whole different way home that took them 20 miles out of the way. Pete's grandpa told his dad to never tell anyone about what they had seen. They even went as far as to lie to his grandmother, saying his dad got bucked off the horse, broke his arm and hit his head on a rock. Pete explained to my grandfather how his dad told him this story on his deathbed to warn him in case he ever smelled that distinct odor while in the woods. His dad never went deep into the woods for the rest of his life. After hearing this my grandpa told Pete he was getting the hell out of there and he didn't want anything to do with these "Wooley Boogers." They left immediately while there was still enough light to see.

This story was my first REAL initiation into the world of Bigfoot, and I must say it scared the living hell out of me as well, because my grandfather was not the type of man to tell you something to simply scare you. Everything we were told was used as a teaching tool and a way of warning us of what to look out for, especially in the deep woods of West Virginia. After awhile I chalked it up as just a story, a way of scaring us kids into listening — until the day came when I saw exactly what they were talking about.

My First Encounter
Gauley River, West Virginia

A long time ago I made a promise, a promise I have now decided to break in order to share this account with all of you. It was a warm midsummer afternoon, and I was beside myself with anticipation on what was about to transpire. I was about to embark on a two day fishing trip with my paternal grandfather, Reverend Oscar Spinks. We had planned to camp out and go fishing at one of our favorite spots on the Gauley River in Nicholas County, West Virginia. The year was 1983.

We arrived at our spot around 2pm and began to unload all of our gear, Grandpa told me go gather up some firewood while he started setting up our tent. We then began getting all of our fishing gear organized and bait prepped for the start of our fishing later in the evening. After all of our gear was stowed and everything just right we decided to take a break and grab a sandwich and soda. I asked Grandpa if I could please put a line in the water — just in case — while we ate our sandwiches. I was so anxious to catch that first fish I could hardly contain myself. He laughed because he knew how excited I was and told me to go ahead and cast a line. I was so excited I was shaking as I tried to get the worm on the hook, and after a few seconds that felt like an eternity, I finally got the bait on the hook and casted out into the river. The line hit the water and I waited as it sank to the bottom. Once I was sure my sinker hit the bottom, I gave it a few cranks to get the line nice and tight, and I set my pole down in the sand on my homemade pole holder. I then went back over to my chair right next to my Grandpa and sat down to get at my sandwich, all the while making sure I kept a keen eye on my pole and line to make sure I wasn't getting a bite.

I was so happy to be spending this time with my grandfather, we ate and drank our soda's and joked with one another about who was going to catch the biggest fish. After some time, I hadn't gotten a bite so Grandpa told me to reel in my line and check my bait. I reeled it in and sure enough my bait was gone so I put another worm on the hook and recast my line, only this time I gave it a big throw and made it out into the middle of the river, even my grandfather made a comment on how far I cast. I set my pole and went over and grabbed my chair to sit closer to my pole. Grandpa grabbed his tackle and went down away from me about fifty yards. After only a few minutes I noticed my line straighten and my pole jerk down violently, I sprang from my chair, grabbed my pole all in one motion and set the hook. The fight was on, and I had hooked a big one.

I yelled with excitement at my grandfather, "I got one! I got one!" Grandpa came running back, barking instructions at me so I wouldn't overreact and lose the fish. I reeled feverishly as the monster trout jumped completely out of the water. After what felt like an hour I dragged the monster rainbow up to the bank and Grandpa snatched it up with the net. I'll never forget what he said. "Boy you got a real nice one there." My trip was a success already, not only did I catch the first fish, I managed to land what would be the biggest trout of the day.

Cast after cast we were catching fish. After we both caught our limit, we continued fishing for a while, catching and releasing. It was now about 6pm and Grandpa said we better get our fire going so we could cook some of our catch. We retrieved our lines and began to prep the fish for the nights supper. As Grandpa got the fish all prepped he told me to peel some potatoes and open up a can of pork and beans. We cooked up the potatoes, trout and beans and ate like kings that evening. I remember I was so full I could hardly move. The sun had begun to set and I threw another log on the fire as we relaxed and enjoyed the wilderness and talked of the days catch.

A huge splash out in the middle of the river startled us. We both jumped to our feet looking in the direction of the ruckus, wondering what could possibly have made a splash that big. I asked Grandpa what he thought it was, and I'll never forget the puzzled look on his face when he said "I'm not sure Dave." We looked up and down the riverbank and saw no sign of anyone or anything. Grandpa yelled out "is anyone there?" No answer. Again he yelled out "is anyone there?" And again, no answer.

As we started to relax and chalk it up as nothing, I heard something very large crashing through the trees, and then I saw what I can only describe as a very large boulder flying up and out of the trees about 20 feet in the air. It seemed to be happening in slow motion and the boulder hit the water with a tremendous, heavy splash. Grandpa yelled for me to get to the truck as he ran to the tent to grab his shotgun. He yelled out facing the direction the boulders came from, "You heathens better get out of here or I will shoot!" and I watched him rack a round into the chamber of the shotgun.

All I heard was silence as I crouched behind the tire of the truck, peeking around toward the other side of the river. Grandpa took aim up high in the air, and fired a shot to scare off whomever or whatever had thrown the boulders our way. The shot rang out like a clap of thunder and echoed through the mountains. When the sound faded, the woods went totally silent, but only for a second or two, and then I heard a sound I will never forget for the rest of my life. The most bone-chilling guttural howl came from across the river where the boulders had come from. It was then I first saw the look of fear on Grandpa's face. This was a man who'd survived the second wave of D-Day as a combat medic, and he was strong in his faith with God. I didn't think he was afraid of anything — until now. Seeing him afraid scared me to death and I began to shake from my head to my toes.

Grandpa raised the shotgun and fired another shot in the

direction of the unearthly howl. Immediately another thunderous howl emerged, even louder than the first, and I cringed in fright as something went crashing through the trees up and away from us. I struggled against fear to try and get a look at what was causing all the ruckus, and could make out what appeared to be a giant, hairy silhouette of a man moving upwards and away from us, only it was much larger than any man I have ever seen in my life. It had very wide muscular shoulders, very long arms and a huge head.

As the creature was moving away from us Grandpa came running over to me and yelled for me to get into the truck. When we both jumped in and sped off my Grandpa said "this is not of God." I shuddered all over and hid my head in my hands. I didn't go back into those woods for many years after that. Grandpa swore me to secrecy about what transpired, and I never spoke of that day when we encountered the West Virginia Stone Man.

My Grandfather passed away in 2016, and it was only then I decided to share our encounter. I first told the story to my uncle Stanton so there would be no misconceptions once the story became public. While telling him of the experience, to my surprise he revealed that Grandpa had come clean with him about it some 25 years earlier. He said Grandpa came to him in obvious distress, wanting to tell him something, but he didn't want Stanton to think he was crazy or drinking, especially with him being a man of the cloth. He had a flock to attend to and didn't want the wild story to circulate to the masses. He told Stanton of how it had been weighing heavily upon him, and he wanted his family to know there were things in the woods we just don't understand.

Stanton said Grandpa not only had the initial encounter with me, he had a second experience not quite two years later, and near the same location. He said Grandpa had gone out fishing again on the Gauley, and as he was walking along a trail he heard a grunting noise, and when he looked up he saw a small "monkey man" as he called them, up in a tree. When they made eye contact it let out a scream similar to what he and I had heard, but not quite as deep. He told Stanton that it scared him to death, and he almost lost his balance in fear. He then heard another one let out a yell from up above the other Monkey Man. He told Stanton that he thought the one in the tree was a young one, and that perhaps an adult was calling out to the young one. He gathered himself up, took a few deep breaths and then backed out off of the trail very slowly, never taking his eyes off the one in the tree until he was no longer able to see it. He then turned and ran to his vehicle and high tailed it out of there. I sat there with the phone in my hand, dumbfounded as I listened to my uncle. When he finished I started to speak, but my uncle stopped me and said "that's not all."

He said that my uncle George on my grandmothers side of the family also had an encounter, in the same area while cutting firewood, and within the same year. Uncle George said that while cutting firewood along the river bank, rocks started flying out of the trees at him, accompanied with very loud screaming and something shaking the dickens out of the brush and Laurel bushes not forty yards from him. George said after he heard those screams he thought he was going to have a heart attack, so he grabbed his chainsaw and busted ass out of there, falling down several times on the way. He also said he never went back there to cut firewood.

Upon hearing yet another story about one of my family members having an encounter in virtually the same area as I did, all I could do was sit in bewilderment for a few, long seconds. As I sat there trying to figure out what to say, Stanton went into yet another story that dealt with him and two of his long time friends in approximately the same area.

He said there was an old moonshiner cave near the river that he and his two friends, Birdie and Squirrelly, would camp out in during the summer months. It was near the river and they loved to go fishing, swimming and camping there. He said they'd been swimming all day, had a few beers and a great time. They had a nice fire going at the mouth of the cave, and were winding down for the night when out of nowhere they heard the most god-awful screaming coming out of the woods, he compared it to a woman being murdered. They all jumped up and looked at each other in shocked wonder. After a few moments the screaming stopped, and Birdie grabbed up his shotgun. Stanton described how all three of them were scared to death, and really didn't know what to do, but began to discuss how they wanted to get the hell out of there.

The screaming started again — only this time it was even closer — and Birdie lost it. He began to fire indiscriminately into the woods, screaming "let's get the hell out of here," then grabbed some of their stuff and sprinted back to the vehicle, never to return to the old moonshiners cave. Stanton said "I will never go back." This for me was shocking and intriguing at the same time. I'd just heard several encounters from immediate family that I never knew anything about, until I decided to tell about our encounter with the West Virginia Bigfoot.

That day on the Gauley River literally changed my life. It compelled me to read and learn all I could get my hands on about other claims of these strange creature encounters. I later went into the military and law enforcement, and became highly trained in self defense, and thoroughly pursued rigid investigation techniques — all pursuits brought on by this bizarre encounter. Over the years I have amassed numerous reports from people of different professional back rounds, age groups and cultural belief systems that describe a large, hairy, bipedal humanoid lurking in the woods of West Virginia. The following are a few of those stories.

Debbie Overbaugh Bond Encounter Near Richwood
Nicholas County, West Virginia

I've known Debbie for several years, and she knew I had been pursuing many cases of reported Bigfoot sightings in our home state. She had mentioned in passing that as a young girl she had indeed experienced something that still terrified her to this day. I was intrigued and asked if I could interview her at a later date. She agreed, and this is her story.

In the Early 1970's Debbie would often spend time at her aunt and uncle's house near Camp Splinter, just outside of Richwood, West Virginia. She recalled hearing her aunt talk about strange happenings around the house, and would often complain to her husband that someone or something was trying to get into the house. She also believed that something would follow behind her car when going into town, and at other times when coming home. It was always in the late evening and at night, and she never saw anything for certain, but she swore something was there. Everyone in the family would tease her about the "monster" that had a crush on her.

The house was approximately a mile from any other homes and

was surrounded by thick woods. Late in the evening during one of Debbie's visits, they decided to make a run into town for some snacks and beverages for her uncle. Her aunt proclaimed that she was not going alone, because of the feelings of being followed previously. She loaded the kids up in the car and headed into town without incident. On the return trip from the store, the kids were all piled in the back seat of the car, laughing, joking and having a good time, without a care in the world. Debbie was sitting directly behind her aunt who was driving, one cousin to her right and another cousin in the front passenger seat. Out of nowhere her aunt yelled "Oh shit!" and stomped on the gas pedal. Debbie said her aunt had a terrified look on her face reflected in the rearview mirror. Debbie then turned her head to the left to try and see what her aunt was looking at, and all she could see was a large, humanoid figure covered in thick, reddish-brown hair from the knee area up to mid-chest. It was running next to and keeping up with the pace of the car. The other kids saw also saw it and became frantic, screaming as her aunt gave the car even more gas.

They came flying into the driveway of the house and jumped out of the car, leaving the car doors open as they all sprinted into the house, crying and screaming to the men folk about what they had seen. The men didn't seem too interested and tried to calm them down by telling them it was probably a bear. The aunt and kids were defiant to this suggestion, claiming a bear doesn't run on two legs and couldn't keep up with the car — even if it was on two legs. The aunt was very distraught and so were Debbie and the cousins. Not two weeks later the family moved from the house never to return. Debbie described her encounter as absolutely terrifying. She remembers it today as if it happened just yesterday. She also told of many other folks around that same time that witnessed a large, hairy creature walking on two legs like a man around the Camp Splinter area.

The Monroe Watchman covers Sasquatch

Cookie Cole Encounters
Monroe County, West Virginia

Cookie is a local farmer whom I met through some friends during one of my investigations in Monroe County. She is a very down to earth and kind person and a pleasure to talk to. Soon after meeting Cookie I was surprised to find out about her numerous encounters with Bigfoot on her property. Cookie described her first experience of seeing a Bigfoot on her property in 1992, while guiding the power company to a set of power lines that ran across her property. She'd wanted the lines moved underground, in order to move her home to another section of the property, away from the main road and it's noise.

Her and the power man loaded up in her Chevy pickup truck and headed up the mountain to the site of the power lines. As they got closer to one of the power poles, Cookie noticed what she thought to be a big, black dog next to the power pole. She thought it was odd looking, and was very intrigued as to what it was, and began to speed up to get a better look at the creature. The power worker hadn't noticed anything yet because he was doing some paper work while she drove. As they approached it, it started to stand up on two legs, and Cookie immediately knew it wasn't a dog, but instead more likely a really big bear.

She continued to speed up and once she got within approximately fifty yards the creature had come to a full and complete upright position, and it was then she realized that it was in fact a great big ape-like looking creature, and it was looking dead at her. Upon making eye contact Cookie described it as turning and taking three giant strides, then wandered over a hill, back through the woods and disappeared from sight. At that point Cookie was going extremely fast and before she even realized it she was off the road and into the field in pursuit of the creature, the truck bouncing around wildly on the uneven surface of the field. She was so intent on regaining sight of what she'd just witnessed that she forgot all about the poor power man sitting in the truck next to her, and looked over and asked him if he had seen it. His face was pale and his eyes were as big as saucers, his paperwork scattered all over the floor. He had one hand on the ceiling to ward off the bouncing ride, and said "Seen what?" Clearly the man did not want to say aloud what they had both seen. Cookie described her first experience as life changing, and would never forget it for the rest of her life.

Another encounter Cookie had occurred October 28th, 2000 at midnight during a full moon. It had not been a good day, according to Cookie. She had to have her Australian Shepherd put to sleep, and had spent most of the day weeping beside the grave of her beloved dog "Sammy." After her friends had left for the night, she sat down in her recliner to try and enjoy a milkshake. She eventually dozed off, and when she awoke she saw what she described as a very large ape, squatting down with its face pressed against the window of her sliding glass door, right in front of her. She was very startled for a few seconds, as one could imagine, waking up and seeing this enormous creature not more than four feet away from where she sat, and only a glass door between it and her.

She said the creature had a head approximately two and a half times wider and two times longer than a normal man's. The face had no hair and was a grey color with a texture similar to a horses nose, with large black eyes just like a cow. After a few seconds she came to her senses and realized she better grab her .38 pistol from off of the refrigerator. She slowly stood and backed up, never taking her eyes off the creature until she got close enough to retrieve her pistol. When she got close enough she spun around and grabbed the gun, taking her eyes off of the creature for roughly one to two seconds, but when she spun back around the creature was nowhere to be seen. Cookie said one thing she could not figure out was how the creature didn't set off her motion-activated light that hangs near the sliding glass window. It didn't turn on when the creature appeared or when it left, and the light was working just fine. According to Cookie these events changed her life. She put non see thru curtains on every one of her windows, and her pistol is never more than an arm's reach away from her at any given time.

Mysterious Prints near Salt Sulphur Springs

Bill Parker Tracks
Monroe County, West Virginia 2015

In the Early afternoon of February 24th, 2015, Bill Parker of Monroe County walked out of his house after a snowy night and discovered a strange set of foot prints in the 12 inch deep snow that had fallen the day before. He was very puzzled as to who could have walked through his yard in the rural area of Salt Sulphur Springs. Upon closer inspection of the tracks he noticed them to be one set of single tracks coming from the hard road in front of his house, up a steep bank and to the right of his place. He noticed that the stride between the tracks seemed to be particularly far apart and measured many of them. Most of the tracks were between 68 and 70 inches apart, the largest being 75 inches from heel to toe. The tracks continued along the side of his house until they came to a clothesline, where it appeared to make who or whatever was making the tracks alter its course to negotiate the obstacle. It appeared as if something or someone physically lifted the clothes line up to get beneath it.

Upon more inspection Bill noticed a clump of hair that was stuck to the line, and a wooden clothespin had been damaged that was not damaged before this incident. The tracks continued under the clothesline, with only a slight deviation from the original path, continuing up the hill of his back yard and into the woods. Wanting to get an idea of what or who may have trekked through his yard, Bill called in some other folks to help him try and Identify what exactly had crossed his property. Neighbor Cookie was called over, as well as a local Sheriff's Deputy, Sean Crosier. The tracks were followed up into the woods until they could be followed no more. The hair was collected and sent off to a lab in order to attempt to get a DNA sample, with results still pending.

Local Veterinarians were also called in to try and Identify the tracks, both confirming that the impressions were made by a bipedal creature. Casts were made of two of the better tracks, but making casts in the snow is very difficult, to say the least. Upon interviewing Bill I discovered that he often hears strange noises coming from the woods behind his house, such as wood knocking, unexplained howls and unexplainable screams. His son verified that he has also heard similar noises, and they both seemed a little unnerved at the fact that they did not know what was causing all these strange happenings around their home, as well as to other neighbors in the area. I asked Bill and his son if they had ever seen a Bigfoot and both said no. Bill himself seems quite skeptical of the notion of Bigfoot existing, let alone of one being on his property. Yet he cannot discount that something unknown, with a huge stride-length made its way across his rural property and left a strange tuft of hair stuck to his clothesline.

Tracks in snow leave citizens puzzled

For the more skeptically-minded folks out there that may dwell in larger metropolitan areas, or for those who simply don't believe a creature such as Bigfoot could be living among us without going unnoticed, let me tell you a little bit more about West Virginia. The entire state is mountainous, the average elevation is 1500 feet above sea level. Forests cover 12 million acres of the state's 15.4 million acres, and it is the third most heavily forested state in the nation, behind only New Hampshire and Maine. There are literally places in the state that man hasn't set foot on in a hundred years — or ever — due to the ruggedness of the terrain. The state is littered with caves that could be used for cover and concealment. There is an over abundance of wild game, such as Whitetail deer, rabbits, grouse and squirrels — just to name a few, not to mention the many domestic animals and farms that could serve as viable food sources for a large animal such as a Bigfoot. West Virginia also boasts an estimated 57,000 acres of wetlands, 40,585 acres of lakes, and 68,139 acres of rivers with numerous species of sustainable aquatic wildlife.

It is also a host to various types of edible plant life such as morels, mushrooms, cattails, ramps, wild onions, berries, acorns, Highland plantain, black walnuts, hazelnuts, beechnuts, apple trees, cherry trees, plums, pears and more. Needless to say there is more than enough habitat to support a large bipedal creature similar to a man or ape within the state. Recorded sightings in the region go back into the 1700s by early European settlers, but Native American legends go back thousands of years and have been passed down generation after generation.

The Cherokee names for Bigfoot are "Tsul Kalu" (slant-eyed giant) and "Nun'yunu' wi (stone man). Indigenous peoples occupied North America for thousands of years before Europeans arrived, and have various names for large, hairy giants that walk on two legs. They have varying legends and tales of the creatures, but the general descriptions are very similar in nature. There are literally hundreds of modern day sightings reported on various websites and publications from all over the Mountain State. Just imagine how many sightings and experiences go unreported for fear of being labeled as crazy by the public? As a general rule most West Virginians are very friendly in nature, however a large part of the population is religious-based, and when it comes to reporting things of the supernatural realm, it is simply something not spoken of. There are new species being discovered every day around the world, and if one was to think about that for just one second with an open mind, the possibility exists that there is a large yet undiscovered Hominid roaming the mountains of West Virginia. I know what I saw and for me there is no doubt about it.

I have often been asked why Bigfoot is not seen more often. There is not a simple answer to this question, but I will offer up a few explanations as to why this may be the case. Most reported sightings have occurred at night or in low light conditions, such as early dawn or late evening, and it is believed by many that Bigfoot is a nocturnal creature. Most humans are sleeping during the night, thus less of a chance to have an encounter with a Bigfoot. Secondly the majority of people live in densely populated areas which would typically not serve a creature such as Bigfoot very well.

Moreover most people simply do not pay attention to their surroundings, they are busy worrying about the kids, the job, talking on their cell phone and in general just going about their day. In the military and law enforcement you are trained to pay attention to your surroundings at all times, always scanning what's in your immediate area, and once you receive this type of training it becomes almost second nature. It soon became very apparent to me how little most people pay attention to what's around them. I often tell people I could hide behind a tree in broad daylight 20 yards away from you and you would never know I was there. So it is common sense that an animal with some level of intelligence such as a Bigfoot could do the same and you would never know it was there. Most encounters and sightings are what I would call an accidental or random occurrence, such as a Bigfoot crossing the road in front of a car at night.

There is also the question of why hasn't there ever been a body found in the woods? There are some answers to that question, as well as some unproven theories. The first being that in a wilderness environment a carcass of an animal will simply not last that long, scavengers and insects will make short work of a carcass within days or weeks. There is also a theory that Bigfoot may indeed bury their dead, obviously not a proven hypothesis. No matter if you fall into the believer category, non-believer or simply just not sure, the fact remains there are thousands of reports from people of all walks of life that have seen a large hairy giant walking on two legs that hasn't yet been proven to exist by modern day science. Some say it's an inter dimensional being. Native Americans believe it is a magical being that can appear and disappear at will, and will show itself to you if you are worthy. Still others believe Bigfoot to be some sort of alien being.

As for me I know what I saw that day with my grandfather. It was a living, breathing creature that walked on two legs just like a man — and it was pissed off! My sole purpose in looking for answers to one of mans greatest questions, (are there unknown creatures walking among us?) was a direct result of the encounter I had that day with my grandfather.

I have conducted many interviews, investigated numerous reported sightings over the years and even spent many nights camping in remote mountainous areas in my search for the West Virginia Bigfoot. Although hard scientific evidence is still lacking at this point, I have come across some interesting foot tracks, heard unexplained tree knocking, and loud screams coming from very remote areas during the night, as well as numerous eyewitness accounts from credible people from all across the state. I have interviewed park rangers, hunters, police officers, doctors, children and lawyers, just to name a few. One can only come to the conclusion that most of them, if not all, have seen something that they can only identify as a Bigfoot. For many the experience was life altering to some degree, some vow to never go into the woods again, others who never carried firearms before now find themselves carrying one on the off chance they ever happen upon Bigfoot again. Families have even picked up and moved to a completely different state because of their encounter. Still others have some have lasting effects many years afterwards, to include frequent nightmares or an intense fear of having another encounter. As for me, my encounter had a profound effect, and led me into a search for answers that has grown into a full blown pursuit of finding evidence that these creatures do in fact exist. More recently I have begun to share and collaborate some of my findings and accounts with other Bigfoot researchers both locally and abroad, in hopes to gain more knowledge in the study of this phenomena. It becomes more apparent when talking with other investigators just how widespread and global the Bigfoot phenomena is.

Spinks checking in with Base Camp

I for one can't help but feel the excitement in the hopes that one day the mystery of this elusive creature will be solved. Perhaps the definitive answers will unveil themselves from the hills and hollows of Wild and Wooly West Virginia.

The Chestnut Ridge Encounters
by Eric Altman

When it comes to places of unusual phenomenon and mysterious creature sightings, Pennsylvania is often overlooked as one of those states. However, nothing could be further from the truth. Not many people are aware of the long, rich history of stories, tales and legends of the supernatural, odd occurrences and strange creatures that haunt the Keystone state.

The history of such tales and legends date back to many of the Native American tribes that called Pennsylvania home. Tribes like the Susquehannock, the Lenni Lenape and the Iroquois all had such stories deep within their tradition. Yes, Pennsylvania is indeed a strange and wondrous place chock full of mysteries waiting to be explored.

One such mystery that holds high esteem with those who seek answers to life's great mysteries is that of weird creature and animal encounters and sightings. Once again, Pennsylvania has that long history of people claiming to have these strange encounters and sightings. These types of sightings and encounters in the Keystone state top the list of strange and unnatural phenomenon.

If we look back to our ancestors, the Native American tribes held such strange creatures sacred in their legends and lore. Creatures like the "Ot-ne-yar-hed" or "Stonish Giant," "The Albeitwitch," a four-foot-tall man-like creature, "The Mesingwi," the guardian of the forest, and the "Thunderbird" are just a few of the mysterious and unusual creatures that were part of the culture and history of our Native

Ancestors.

The creature we more commonly know as Bigfoot or Sasquatch also has a history in the state that dates back hundreds of years. The earliest documented newspaper account on file for Pennsylvania dates to August 4, 1838. It appeared in the *Bangor Daily Whig and Courier Newspaper* out of Bangor, Maine. The article was entitled "The Whistling Wild Boy of the woods." The article recounted the tale of a strange encounter a young man had with a small, 4-foot-tall, hair-covered, upright walking creature that occurred the year prior near Bridgewater in Silver Lake Township near the Pennsylvania and New York state line. Since that first article in 1838, hundreds of newspaper stories and magazine articles have documented claims of encounters and sightings of strange, man-like beasts and creatures across the Keystone state.

Pennsylvania is a strange place indeed. What makes the state even more fascinating is the fact there are areas within the state that are well documented and known for their various types of phenomenon. Gettysburg, for example, is well known and recognized for its haunted battlefields and countless historic locations. The northern forested region of the state is known for reports of the large flying cryptid known as the Thunderbird. UFO sightings have been commonly sighted and reported in the far eastern counties of the state. Pennsylvania seems to have its own little pockets of areas of strange and mysterious phenomenon. One area seems to encompass all facets of the supernatural. This area come to be known as a hot bed of this type activity year after year, and never disappoints when it comes to the strange and supernatural. The area is found in the Southwestern corner of the state and is called the Chestnut Ridge.

The Chestnut Ridge is the westernmost ridge in the Appalachian Mountains. It is primarily part of the Laurel Highlands region of southwestern Pennsylvania. The Ridge rises in southern Indiana County, and continues in a southwesterly direction for over 100 miles through Westmoreland and Fayette Counties, before crossing into West Virginia, then gradually slopes down, ending 10 miles southeast of Morgantown in Preston County.

Chestnut Ridge, Fayette County

Much like the rest of the state, the Chestnut ridge is no stranger to a long history of strange and unusual phenomenon. The unusual activity on the Ridge dates back decades and covers the gamut of a wide variety of strange phenomenon. During the 1980's a Philadelphia newspaper reporter wrote about the Ridge, calling it the "Twilight Zone of Pennsylvania" due to the number of strange events reported. That includes UFO's, weird lights in the sky, creature sightings, hauntings and other anomalous phenomenon. Fayette County, being one of those counties the Chestnut Ridge runs through also has its share of these strange occurrences, which include a high number of bizarre creature reports. Its geography, ample habitat and abundant wildlife make it a perfect place for animals both discovered and undiscovered to live and survive in, with little or no interaction with the residents who live there. Fayette County sits in southwestern Pennsylvania, adjacent to Maryland and West Virginia. As of the 2010 census, the population was 136,606. The county was created on September 26, 1783, from part of Westmoreland County and named after the Marquis de Lafayette.

The first Europeans in Fayette County were explorers who had used an ancient American Indian trail that bisected the county on their journey across the Appalachian Mountains. In 1754, 22-year-old

George Washington fought against the French at Jumonville Glen and Fort Necessity. British forces under Washington and General Edward Braddock improved roads throughout the region, making the future Fayette County an important supply route.

According to the U.S. Census Bureau, the county has a total area of 798 square miles, of which 790 square miles is land and 8 square miles is water. The western portion of the county contains rolling foothills and two valleys along the Monongahela and Youghiogheny rivers. The eastern portion of the county is highly mountainous and forested, with many coal mines and caves located within the area. Fayette County is well known for its outdoor recreation opportunities which include hiking, hunting, camping and fishing, thanks in part to the Forbes State Forest, which covers a good portion of the county and the vast forested area of the Chestnut Ridge. There is also an abundance of wildlife and game in the area, which includes a healthy number of deer, black bear, fox, and coyotes, among other common wild life.

The Bigfoot sightings in the Chestnut Ridge area are also a commonplace occurrence and reported on a yearly basis. As with most phenomena, the activity seems to come in waves. Some years there is a rise in reports and activity and others the activity is slow and often less reported. Regardless of the annual volume, the activity continues year after year and the Bigfoot activity and sightings never stop.

The first known encounter in Fayette County was recorded in the early 1920's when a young woman had strange encounters with what she called "hairy wild men" in the small village of Indian Head. From that point forward, Bigfoot sightings have been reported over the years to various researchers and the news media. One such Pennsylvania researcher has dedicated the majority of his life investigating claims of the strange and unusual in Pennsylvania. Beginning in 1958, fortean researcher Stan Gordon investigated hundreds of such claims during his long 57 year career, and has talked to as many if not more eyewitnesses claiming such encounters.

During the early part of the 1970's, Stan and his research group were heavily involved in investigating cases which are now known as part of the 1973 and 1974 flap of Bigfoot and UFO sightings in Pennsylvania. Most of the reports were recorded along the Chestnut Ridge in Westmoreland and Fayette County. Stan and his group investigated hundreds of cases during that two year period. There has never been anything before or after the flap of 1973 and 1974 in regards to the sheer number of reported and documented sightings. As Stan has been quoted saying, "if I hadn't been involved in investigating the cases, I would have never believed it had occurred." In recent years, Stan has written multiple books on his research investigating the cases during the 1973 and 1974 flap along with other strange cases in Pennsylvania. Residents and visitors to Fayette County have continued to report sightings and encounters to Gordon and other researchers in the area. However, there has been nothing quite like the flap that occurred in the early 1970's. Stan continues to this day investigating these cases, although primarily on his own.

My name is Eric Altman. I am what some would call a Cryptozoologist, a Bigfoot researcher or an enthusiast. I simply call myself someone who is very interested in the Bigfoot phenomenon. I have been studying a variety of paranormal topics since I was 10 years old. My interest in Bigfoot began in 1980 when I saw the films "Legend of Boggy Creek" and "Creature from Black Lake." I have been actively studying the subject matter for over 36 years and investigating cases for 20 years. I've led countless expeditions, investigated hundreds of cases and have lectured across the country for over 16 years. Although I don't consider myself an expert by any means, I feel I have a fairly good understanding of the subject matter of Bigfoot, especially when it comes to the phenomenon and history in Pennsylvania. In 1997, when I began actively investigating cases and reports, I was already familiar with Stan Gordon's work. Stan was my mentor, as I had been studying his research and the historical reports of Pennsylvania that had occurred, especially in the Chestnut Ridge area.

During the past 20 years, Stan and I have had the pleasure of working closely together and investigating cases throughout the state. However, things would change for me between the years 2009 and 2011, as Stan and I would have the opportunity to return to the Fayette County area to work together and investigate a series of reports which came to be known as the Fayette flap of 2009 to 2011.

During the summer of 2009, I was the acting Director of the Pennsylvania Bigfoot Society. It was a group of about 75 men and women volunteering their time and efforts investigating reported sightings, encounters and claims. Our members were made up of individuals with a variety of different skill sets and vocational backgrounds in various fields. Most brought varying levels of knowledge and experience in wildlife and the outdoors to the group. At that time, I had been actively involved in working within the Bigfoot community and working with many other researchers and research groups. I had established a large network of contacts with those researchers and groups across the country, sharing information and reports.

The Fayette Flap of sightings began in the summer of 2009 and came to an end in the fall of 2011. The Pennsylvania Bigfoot Society, Stan Gordon and other independent researchers were involved in investigating countless reports of alleged sightings, audible claims, foot print discoveries, and other strange occurrences throughout the county. We investigated as many of the reports as we were able to. Some of the reports were simply that, reports submitted to the group with nothing more to follow up on. Some of the cases reported yielded no evidence during the follow up investigation, while others were nothing more than fabrications meant to send us on a wild goose chase. The flap kept the PA Bigfoot Society quite busy documenting, investigating and following up quite a number of claims and reports. I've decided to share a handful of the more interesting cases from that time. Included are some of the results of the investigations we conducted, along with some of the personal experiences and evidence we were able to document and record. Some of these cases were included in newspaper articles and on season 7 of the television show Finding Bigfoot.

It was July 10th, 2009, when the first report was submitted and appeared to set off a wave of sightings over the course of the next few years in Fayette County. After her sighting, the witness went online and searched for someone to help answer what it may have been that she experienced. She discovered the Sasquatch Watch of Virginia website and submitted her encounter. Billy Willard, who was the Director at that time, forwarded her information and report off to the Pennsylvania Bigfoot Society to investigate. I spoke with the witness by phone and received a summary of what she encountered. During the phone conversation, the witness agreed to meet with a small research team on July 16th. The team was composed of Stan Gordon, David and Cindy Dragosin of the PA Bigfoot Society and myself. David and Cindy were vital to the investigation because both were former residents of the neighborhood, and very familiar with the location and area in general.

We met with the witness and her husband at the Rite Aid Pharmacy on Connellsville Street directly across from Lafeyette School where the incident occurred on July 10th.

Rite Aid Pharmacy, Uniontown, PA

After a brief introduction, the witness walked us to the exact location where the incident occurred and began to recount her experience with us. It was approximately 6:00 PM on the evening of July 10th. The weather conditions were warm and clear. The witness was driving north on Connellsville Street, about 35 to 40 miles an hour when suddenly, she caught out of the corner of her eye, a figure quickly approaching her direction from her left side. The woman initially thought it was a person who was going to run into the road directly in front of her car. To avoid the oncoming collision, she immediately swerved her car to the curb on the right and came to an abrupt stop. That's when she got a good look at the figure and realized it was not a person, but a strange, hair-covered creature. She expected the creature to continue to cross in front of her car, and sat there for a few seconds, but it didn't happen. The woman looked into her rear view mirror, realizing that the creature had changed direction and gotten behind her. "I looked into the rear view mirror and I saw it leap across my trunk," the woman stated.

She sat in her car trying to regain her composure. She could not believe what had just occurred. Seconds later she looked up to see the creature now on her right side, running quickly away from her car down the middle of another road about 75 feet away. That was the last time she saw it. The entire incident lasted just several seconds, but enough time for the witness to recall a detailed description of a creature which she was certain was not human, or a person in a costume.

She described what she saw in daylight and at very close range as a dark-colored, hair-covered, man-like creature. She estimated it was, "at least 6 feet tall or slightly taller." The creature, which walked upright on two legs, had a head that was said to be large and elongated, and covered with hair that looked wild and disheveled.

The neck was somewhat hard to see since it was covered in hair, however, the witness said it appeared to be thin and long. She remarked that the neck looked strange because the head was big and the shoulders were wide. She added the face was mainly covered in hair, yet the area that was exposed appeared to be very white. She went onto explain that there was hair coming out from all over the face, like that of a dog or a wolf, and that the nose was flat and dark, but was also mostly covered in hair. The mouth and ears were not seen since they were covered with hair as well.

The eyes were the most prominent feature that caught the witnesses' attention. She described the eyes as circular in shape and at least twice the size of a human. They were wide set, dark, possibly black in color, and wild looking. The witness could see no iris, or whites of the eyes. The witness also stated the creature had a wild look in its eyes that frightened her.

The woman went on to describe the build of the creature as stocky and muscular in appearance. The chest area was described as thick and hairy. The shoulders were very broad. The arms were very long, and hung down to its knees or just below. The witness said the hair on the arms was also long, much like the hair of an ape. The woman didn't recall seeing any muscles, however, it appeared as though it was well built, and in good physical shape. She had the impression that this creature was younger in age, somewhere between adolescence and adulthood. The witness had her windows up at the time with her air conditioner running, so she was not able to detect any unusual sounds or odors of note during the sighting.

When the witness described the creature, PA Bigfoot Society's Dave Dragosin sketched an illustration of the creature under the direction of the eyewitness. The witness' husband and I searched a wooded area not far from the location of the encounter, but nothing of interest was found.

Sketch of a creature sighted at Camp Carmel September 2009.
Sketch by David Dragosin

Stan examined the car for any evidence or damage that might have been left by the creature during the encounter. While he was looking over the car body, he noticed what appeared to be unusual scratch marks on the trunk surface and on the left side of the vehicle. Stan pointed it out to the others, as well as the woman and her husband. They had never seen this surface area damage before as the car was a new model purchased a short time prior. The scratched area of the trunk measured 6 inches from the left tail light to the first set of scratches. The scratched area was about 8.5 inches long and 2 inches wide. There were numerous vertical and horizontal, very thin scratch lines that went into the paint surface. The researchers speculated there was a possibility the damage may have been related to the creature's movements as it leapt across the trunk area from that side.

It was the research teams impression that the witness was very sincere and competent. She described to the group what she had seen and experienced that night in great detail. It was evident she was still emotionally upset by what had occurred. The witness told Stan that after the encounter, she drove down the road a short distance and parked her car. She sat there thinking about what had happened. She was trying to convince herself that this was a person, but eventually realized it couldn't have been. She came up with her own reasons why she felt what she saw and encountered was not a human. Firstly was the rate of speed the figure came across into the path of her car, it didn't seem to care that it was going to get hit. Secondly was the very fast movement of the creature and the way it leapt over the trunk. She also had a good look at the creature and some of its facial features. The eyes of the creature frightened her.

After the witness arrived home she waited awhile before telling her family about what she had seen. At first she was initially met with some disbelief from her children, but her husband listened to her and believed she had seen something. He suggested she should call the police to see if anyone else had reported something similar. However, she decided not to call the police because she felt she would have been ridiculed.

Since the sighting occurred in front of the Rite Aid Pharmacy, I went into the store to talk to the store manager and anyone in the store that may have been working that night. After a brief conversation, I was told no one in the store had reported anything unusual. The clerk working that night did tell me that there had been a black bear sighting in the school yard a few months prior to the witnesses encounter.

The direction the creature was last observed moving towards would take it into a heavily wooded area in the direction of Jummonville and the Chestnut Ridge. There has been a long history of Bigfoot sightings reported for many years in this same general area of Fayette County. Stan wrote up the investigation summary report and released the information on his website and to the media. A few weeks later both Stan and I were contacted by newspaper reporter Dave Zuchowski from the *Uniontown Herald Standard* of Uniontown, PA. He spoke with both Stan and I about the incident to try and gather more information. He also wanted to interview the witness but she refused to be interviewed or discuss the incident further. On August 24, 2009 the article about the encounter entitled "PA Group probes Bigfoot reports" was released in the Uniontown paper. So began a string of incidents spanning the next three years.

A few days after the article was released, my phone was ringing again. I received a call from one of two twin sisters who resided in the small village of Dunbar, PA. After reading the newspaper article, she was anxious to share her story with me and was hopeful we could provide her with some answers as to what she had experienced on her old homestead property just a few weeks prior.

It was early in the morning of July 28, when the two sisters headed to their old homestead property, a routine they carried out several times throughout the week as caretakers of the old family settlement. It was a small piece of land on which part of the old basement foundation still sat. The property sat on the side of a hill at the base of the Chestnut Ridge, and was surrounded by thick briar and blackberry bushes. A long dirt driveway provided the only access from the main road. The blackberry bushes and briars provided excellent privacy and security from the few surrounding neighbors, and the forested hillside joined at the top of the yard. The small village of Dunbar is one of many small communities in Fayette County that litter the base of the Chestnut Ridge.

Eric Altman checking height measurements

An almost daily ritual, the two sisters would drive over to the old property for lawn maintenance, to pull weeds, do some light landscaping, feed the feral cats and tidy up the property. On that particular morning, the sisters pulled into the long dirt driveway and parked the car. The elder of the two sisters told the younger to wait in the car and she'd return shortly, then went to feed a few of the feral cats and inspect the place. As she got out of the car she walked the remaining length of the dirt driveway. At the end she rounded the edge of the blackberry bushes and entered the yard to her right. As she walked into the yard she came within 40 yards of a small, light beige-colored animal squatted down at the top end of the property, eating from the farthest blackberry bush. She continued to quietly approach the animal thinking it was a small deer. As she got within 30 feet, it stood erect. According to her statement, once the creature stood up it was approximately 3 ½ feet tall. The creature must have heard the woman coming, as it turned very slowly and cautiously, looking back at her where she'd stopped. The creature then quickly turned and bolted south, off into the thick brush and remaining upright on two legs.

The woman was puzzled and confused as to what she'd just witnessed. Standing silently, she tried to make logical sense of the sighting. Suddenly, the sound of rustling brush, breaking branches and snapping twigs grabbed her attention and was growing louder. Her focus was quickly drawn to her left and that's when she saw a second creature. She described it as a "huge, hulking monkey man" that approached her from the blackberry bush. It walked right to the edge of the blackberry bush and then stopped. She and the creature stood and stared at each other for several seconds. The woman and the creature's eyes locked for what seemed an eternity. It then slowly turned and walked back in an easterly direction through the very thick briars and brush, flailing its arms as it made its way deeper into the thicket before disappearing from sight.

It was at that point the woman turned and walked back to the car. She got in and told her sister what she had just seen. They agreed to both keep quiet about what the sister saw, as no one would likely believe them anyway. That was until they read the article in the *Uniontown Herald Standard*. During the course of the phone conversation, both her and her sister agreed to allow a research team to come out to their property, meet with them in person and let them show us the area of the encounter.

A few days later, a research team which consisted of Pennsylvania Bigfoot Society Members Dave and Cindy Dragosin, myself and Independent Researcher Dwayne Pintoff met with the ladies at the old family homestead. We found the sisters to be quite excitable and most willing to share what the elder sister had seen that day in July. They were very eager to show us where the small creature stood and where the larger creature approached her from the blackberry bushes. While pointing out the area, the elder sister was quick to indicate to me a pink flower high in one of the bushes the creature had walked by. She said the head of the creature just cleared beneath the flower as it walked past it. After a 20 minute trek of scratching and tearing through the briars and thorns to get to that spot, I made it back to the point where the pink flower was. The distance from the ground to the pink flower measured 9 feet. A thorough search of the area by the team of investigators found no conclusive evidence. The witness granted Dave Dragosin permission to sketch the larger of the two creatures she had seen.

We did however have an interesting experience on the property a few weeks later. Members of the Pennsylvania Bigfoot Society which included David and Cindy Dragosin and I were sitting out on the property late one night in early September of 2009. It was just past 10 pm. The neighbors who lived on the hill behind the property had returned home and drove up the long driveway adjacent to the property and pulled their car into the garage. Once inside the garage they shut the outside yard light off. It wasn't more than 5 minutes after the neighbors had gone inside that Dave, Cindy and I heard a large tree fall over in the forest, just above the house to the east, 100 yards above the property, right where we were sitting that bordered the neighbor's yard. Usually a tree falling isn't such a strange thing in itself, but within a few minutes, a second tree fell over. No further sounds or incidents were heard that night. Was it a coincidence that two trees fell within minutes of one another or was something not too happy to see the neighbors come home that night?

In the early fall of 2009, sighting reports and claims of encounters continued to come in to the PA Bigfoot Society. In late August 2009, we received another interesting report. This one occurred a few weeks prior in the village of Jumonville that sits up on top of the Chestnut Ridge. The small village of Jumonville consists of a family owned Italian restaurant known as Fabrizi's, a few scattered homes and hunting cabins. The remainder of the village is made up of public and private forested land and state game lands. Jumonville is well known for several things. One of the most recognizable icons is the Jumonville Christian Camp, Retreat Center and Resort that has a historic landmark, a 60 foot high steel cross that on a clear day can be seen from up to 3 states and 50 miles away. Another is the Jumonville Glen, an historic location where the opening battle of the French and Indian War took place on May 28, 1754. There a company of colonial militia from Virginia led by George Washington ambushed a small unit of French Canadian soldiers. Jumonville has also become recognized over the last 50 years as the number of reported Bigfoot sightings and encounters increased in the area. Mainly those that occurred during the 1973 and 74 sighting flap, but have continued up to present day. The report we received from the witness occurred in late August of 2009 and it was one featured in the Fayette County episode of Finding Bigfoot.

What makes this report interesting is not necessarily the location where it occurred but more in regards to the witness who encountered the creature. A woman named Nicki who contacted us was not a native to our country. She had just recently moved to the U.S. from

Amsterdam. She was living in the Uniontown area and working at the Nemacolin Woodlands Resort and Casino several miles away. Nicki worked late nights at the resort and often found herself driving home along the Chestnut Ridge through Jumonville. Her travel route on Jumonville Road is a windy mountain path surrounded by forest on both sides, and is teeming with an abundance of wildlife. She was familiar enough with the road at night, and the chances of frequent wildlife crossing the roadway, that she often chose to drive at reduced speeds for safety reasons.

On the night of August 8, 2009, Nicki had no idea what lie ahead of her on her trip home. As she was driving she could see car tail lights ahead of her in the distance. The car in front of her suddenly braked and made an abrupt left turn into the parking lot of Fabrizi's. The car quickly turned around in the parking lot and sped off on Jumonville Road passing her in the opposite direction. Although she found that strange, she continued driving towards home. As she passed Fabrizi's she began to round the bend in the road. She saw a figure walking ahead of and away from her down the middle of the road. She began to slow down even more as her high beams lit up the figure, bringing more details to light.

At first glance, she thought it was a man walking down the middle of the roadway wearing a heavy fur coat. She coasted up behind the figure slowing to almost a near stop. The figure did not move, so she proceeded to drive her car around the figure to the left to pass. As she did, that is when the figure leaned down and looked right into the windshield at her. She got a very clear look at the face of this creature. It was at that point, she knew she wasn't looking at a person.

Nicki sped up and drove at a very high rate of speed away from the creature. She left the creature standing in the middle of the roadway and never looked back. The next morning she told her boyfriend of the very strange encounter and what she had seen walking down the middle of the road. She did not call what she saw a Bigfoot and really had no name for it. Her boyfriend told her of the number of Bigfoot sightings in the Jumonville area and that is what she probably saw. After discussing it with her boyfriend and reading the article in the newspaper, Nicki decided to contact the PA Bigfoot Society and report her encounter.

Sketch of a creature reported in Jumonville, PA 2009.
Sketch by David Dragosin.

Dave, Cindy Dragosin and I met Nicki at the Fabrizi's parking lot. She recounted her sighting and what she experienced that night. She permitted Dave to sketch the creature based upon the description she gave us. One thing of note is that when asked, she stated she was not familiar with Bigfoot, never had heard of such a creature until her boyfriend told her of the likely culprit. Her initial thoughts were that it was just someone wearing a fur coat and a bad Halloween mask, but when it looked down at her, she knew it most certainly wasn't a person. Dave, Cindy and I examined the bend in the roadway where she saw the creature and did not find any evidence to corroborate her sighting. We felt she was honest and sincere, making her encounter credible. When presented to the producers of Finding Bigfoot, they too agreed and used her sighting for a re-enactment segment of the Fayette County episode in Season 8.

It wasn't long before the PA Bigfoot Society was hot on the trail of another report. This one occurred September 22, 2009, and I was writing up the investigation case report of Nicki's sighting when the phone was ringing again. This time my friend and colleague Stan Gordon was on the other end. Stan relayed an eyewitness contact information and sighting report he had just received from a woman who had just hung up the phone. The woman phoned Stan and reported to him that both she and her daughter had a sighting of a creature a few hours prior to calling him, and wanted to report the incident right away. Stan gathered preliminary information and then called me to contact the witness and assemble a team to investigate. After conversing with Stan, I phoned the witness. She was still very excited and panicked at the same time to talk to someone about what she and her daughter had just witnessed.

It was mid afternoon when Jill and her daughter Bethany decided to go for a drive in the Chestnut Ridge. They wanted to spend an afternoon on some of the back mountain roads that meander through the state game lands. They ended up near Camp Carmel Christian Youth Camp, which sits well off the main roadway on Camp Carmel Road. As they were headed towards Camp Carmel, they crossed a wide gas well line that runs through the area and intersects the road. It is a long gas well, and from their vantage point on the gravel road, you could look out and see for miles to the east and west. The women slowed down to enjoy the view. They also wanted to see if they could spot any deer or other wildlife on the gas well line. After stopping for a few moments and not seeing anything, they decided to continue on. They drove for a little while on the gravel road, then decided to head back home. They found a spot in the roadway to turn around where the old Liston school once stood. As they were headed back they decided to stop one more time at the gas well gate. This time, they parked the car and walked to the head of the gas well road to take in the view.

While Jill and her daughter were standing there enjoying the scenery, a few moments had passed. About 100 yards down the hill on the gas well, they heard branches breaking and brush rustling from inside the tree line on the north side of the gas well. Jill and her daughter fully expected to watch a deer or bear come out of the forest on the left side. However what they saw was not like anything they had ever seen before. They both watched as a tall, dark, hair-covered creature lumbered out of the tree line walking across the gas well from left to right. The creature walked at a fast pace with its arms pumping at its side. Within a matter of seconds the creature had crossed the gas well entering the tree line on the opposite southern side. The creature did not seem to notice the women nor pay attention to them as it crossed, apparently determined to continue on its way, where ever it was going.

After standing at the top of the hill on the road watching for a few moments, the women entered the car and quickly drove off towards home. When they arrived, Jill told all about the sighting to her boyfriend Jeff. At first he didn't believe her, but agreed to return to the area for a look to see if they could spot the creature again, or find any sign of its passage. They returned about an hour later and looked, but saw no further sign of the creature. They drove around a few of the area back roads and did not see any other sign of the animal. After returning home, she made the initial phone call to Stan. During my conversation with Jill, she agreed to meet with me the following morning and take a small investigation team out to the location.

The next morning at 8:00 am, Dave and Cindy Dragosin, my son Josh and I met Jill, Jeff and Jill's daughter. We followed them to Camp Carmel Road and the gas well area where Jill relayed her encounter to Dave, Cindy and I. Jill then showed us where her daughter and she were standing looking down and pointed to where the creature exited the tree line on the left, crossed the gas well line and entered on the right. We walked down the hill to the spot where Jill said the creature exited the tree line. We searched the edge of the eastern tree line and found some interesting signs of something large that had been walking around the brush and high grass. We found large impressions in the high grass, and exactly at the tree line we found a small blackberry bush where something had picked all the blackberries from the stems up high, but left all the blackberries on the stems close to the ground. The grass was trampled and smashed down as if a large animal had been standing or moving around at the blackberry bushes.

We entered the left tree line but could not find any foot prints, impressions or tracks of any kind inside the tree line. The area inside was very hard to maneuver through with thick briars and brambles. Some were so thick we had to find ways around. We searched for about an hour and could not find any sign of a large creature walking on that side of the gas well line.

It was decided we should focus our attention on where Jill had said the creature crossed. We did find multiple used game trails crossing the expanse, but were unable to identify the trail used by the creature. The tree line on the right side of the trail was easier to enter and there were little to no briars inside the tree line. We were able to walk around there more freely.

Casting a track discovered at Camp Carmel September 2009

After an exhaustive search, we only discovered one possible track in a dried up creek bed. The large foot shaped impression measured 19 inches in length, 9 inches wide and an inch and a half deep. Since we found no other impressions or possible tracks, it was decided to cast this one. I returned to the car and gathered the casting material and returned to make a cast of the possible print. After pouring the material, it was decided to leave the material there over the weekend to set and dry properly and I would return on Sunday to collect the print. I did cover the print with plastic material and cardboard to try to protect it from the elements. Jeff, Jill and I continued to search the area further but did not find anything else. When we returned to the vehicles we met Dave, Cindy and Josh there waiting for us.

Jill's daughter had locked herself in the car and refused to get out. Apparently she became quite frightened after returning back to the area, and decided it was safer if she climbed in the car and locked herself in. While I was talking to David, he informed me that while he and Cindy were waiting for us by the parked trucks, they had several loud knocking sounds coming from the three lines on both sides of the gas well behind them. They also heard strange animal calls that seemed to be moving through the forest circling them. The best description they could give for the sounds was that the calls were very similar to the sound of a peacock. Which is odd in itself as peacocks are not native to the state, let alone the Fayette County area. After exploring the area, I informed Jill and Jeff I would return on Sunday to retrieve the cast from the creek bed. Jill thanked us for coming out and we parted ways.

On Sunday afternoon, I met up with Dave, Cindy, Jeff and Jill back at the gas well. They were quite excited to share with me what they discovered while we were gone. On Saturday afternoon, they decided to return to the area and expand their search for signs of the creature, looking for any additional tracks. They decided to hike a dirt trail about 100 yards further northeast of where Jill and her daughter had seen the creature on Thursday afternoon. While they were hiking the dirt trail, they came across an animal kill. They discovered what appeared to be the carcass of a very large domesticated hog. They did not know how it ended up there or what had killed it. There was a strong smell of decay in the air and there was blood around the body, making it evident that other predators had begun to feed on the dead hog.

The body for the most part was still intact. Jeff took a number of photos with his cell phone to document the find. When we talked with them about what they found on Saturday afternoon, Jeff showed me the photos he had taken with his phone confirming it was a large hog. Jeff estimated the hog weighed several hundred pounds based on its size. I mentioned to Jeff that I'd like to take a walk down there before I collected the cast and have a look at the hog. As we approached, we could definitely smell the decaying animal and knew we were getting close. As we rounded the bend in the trail and walked up into the clearing, Jeff stopped and had a puzzled look on his face. There were bits and pieces of flesh and dried, pooled blood stained the ground, but something was missing. The hog was gone.

The five of us stood surprised and baffled that the hog had disappeared within a day. I closely examined the ground and the surrounding area for signs of drag marks, animal tracks, tire tracks, scrapes or anything indicating what may have taken the hog. I found nothing to identify the thief. We hiked back out to the main trail, searched the bushes surrounding the tree line and forest for several hundred feet in all directions, and still found no sign of the hog. We had a second mystery on our hands. Not only did Jill and her daughter see a mysterious creature Thursday afternoon, but the hog Jeff and Jill discovered and photographed was missing. Someone or something carried off the hog. There were no signs that it was drug off, or eaten and scraps were left remaining. The carcass was completely gone with the exception of a few chunks of flesh and dried blood on the ground. We talked for a bit and continued our search, then I walked over to the dried creek bed and retrieved the cast.

It had rained off and on that weekend and despite the attempt to protect the cast from the elements, I was unsuccessful. I dug the cast out of the ground and took it back to the car with me. The cast eventually fell apart because it retained too much water and never set properly. We were never able to say exactly what Jill and her daughter saw on the gas well road that Thursday afternoon. I cannot say the casting I made and retrieved was a cast of a Bigfoot footprint. We could never determine who or what took the dead hog. We left this case as unsolved with lots of questions remaining unanswered. I along with other researchers in the area return to the gas well periodically, to sit and watch for animals crossing and to listen for calls and knocks. Despite the multiple times I've been back up there, I've never seen anything out of the ordinary, nor heard what I could identify as a Bigfoot.

During the fall months and early into winter of 2010, the PA Bigfoot Society continued to follow up on reported road crossings, foot print discoveries, reports of strange animal sounds and other unusual activity. Members of the Society spent a significant time investigating many cases, some of which turned out to be wild goose chases. Some of the cases reported were misidentifications. There were even a few cases we were not able to follow up on because the witness refused to meet with us.

In February 2010 something pretty rare occurred when it comes to Bigfoot sightings. Now, a Bigfoot sighting is considered by many to be a rare event to begin with, but what happened in late January and February 2010 involved two sightings in the same area, under different circumstances, witnessed by different individuals. The two sightings occurred along a small stretch of a two lane road less than a half a mile apart. The two sightings were witnessed weeks apart by two different groups of people who did not know each other. The sightings took place between a section of Ferguson Road and Ferguson Hollow Road outside of Dunbar, PA. Ferguson Road is a two lane paved road with forested area on both sides. Ferguson Hollow Road is a gravel and dirt road that serves as an access road leading back to a remote forest at the base of the Chestnut Ridge, and to an old abandoned stone quarry.

The first sighting occurred on January 27, 2010. It was approximately 9:00 pm when an uncle and nephew were traveling west in a pickup truck along Ferguson Rd. The uncle and nephew had just come down a small hill on Ferguson, and passing Ferguson Hollow Road on their right and were heading up the hill. At that time, there was snow on the ground and visibility was better due to the newly fallen snow.

As they were ascending the hill, without warning a large dark figure emerged from the right side of the roadway into the oncoming path of the truck. The uncle was forced to slam on the brakes. As they sat stopped, they watched as a dark, brown, hair-covered creature exited the culvert on the right side of the roadway, then walked quickly across the road in 3 and ½ steps before entering the tree line on the opposite side. The first assumption was they were seeing a bear step onto the roadway walking on two legs, but quickly realized the creature was much taller than a bear, the arms and legs were out of bear proportions, especially the arms, as they hung down to the knees. The creature never once looked at the truck as it crossed the roadway.

The two men sat momentarily in silence and disbelief. After

regaining their composure, and realizing what they had just witnessed, the uncle then drove home and told his family. He made a few phone calls to a few friends about what they had just seen. Within a short time, a small posse that included family and friends went back to the area to search for tracks and clues to determine what exactly the two men saw. Upon returning, they searched the area and found tracks in the snow on both sides of the roadway.

Much to their surprise, it appeared the tracks lead from the left side of the road and crossed into the tree line on the right. The tracks continued down the culvert and made a large loop coming back up the culvert, then reentered the roadway where the men had watched the creature cross in front of their truck. The uncle also claimed they found several tufts of dark brown hair on a briar bush along the track way heading up the hillside on the left side of the road. Unfortunately, the deep snow made it difficult for the group to continue following the tracks any further so they called off the search.

The following day the Uncle phoned Dave Dragosin and filed his report. Dave set up a date and time on February 5, 2010 for the witnesses to meet with our small investigation team and show us the hair and the location where the sighting took place. Unfortunately for our research team, the men did not meet us that day. They never returned any of our phone calls or attempts to contact them after their initial call to Dave.

Being proactive, our team did go to the location to search the area for any signs or evidence to validate the men's alleged sighting. Not only did the men not meet us, but we were greeted with further bad news. A winter storm added several additional inches to the area and between the date of the initial sighting and our arrival, the snow total was well over 10 inches. Despite our exhaustive search of the area, we were not able to find any tracks or further signs of what the two men reported.

Our research group felt the phoned report sounded somewhat believable. But without the men meeting us and not returning phone calls, we began to lean towards the possibility of the report being nothing more than a wild goose chase. A few days later, a second report was filed that had us rethinking the validity of the report that occurred 10 days prior.

On February 20, 2010, two women were driving east on Ferguson

Road in the late afternoon. As they descended the road, they were about to pass Ferguson Hollow Road on the right. As they slowed down at the bottom of the hill, the passenger looked out her window and down Ferguson Hollow Road. She yelled out to stop the car. The woman driving slammed on her brakes and came to a stop. The passenger told her to back up to Ferguson Hollow Road. When she did, both women looked down the access road. In the middle of the roadway, standing less than 50 yards away, they both saw a tall dark figure. The creature was standing motionless in the middle of the gravel road looking up the wooded hillside. The women sat and watched the figure for several seconds before it began to walk up the hillside into the thick underbrush and out of sight. They sat in the roadway hoping to see more of the creature but it was gone.

When the women reported their sighting, they described the creature as tall and covered in dark brown hair or fur. The arms hung very low and they saw no signs of clothing. They both stated the creature never looked in their direction and walked effortlessly up the hillside. After the phone conversation, the women agreed to meet with us at the sighting location.

The weather had warmed up over the days following their sighting and the snow that blanketed the area melted off. The ground was very wet and muddy making the ground conditions much better for finding tracks. The research team met with the women and they showed us where the creature stood. We searched both the bank leading up to the gravel road and as far up the hillside that we could ascend. Nothing was found where the creature was sighted and walked up the hillside. The team decided to walk further back up Ferguson Hollow Road. We discovered a few interesting things during the walk back into the forest.

While we were walking back on the access road, the team came across a deer carcass lying on the left side of the road. After examining the deer, it was apparent that it was shot and harvested by a hunter. But we discovered there were several odd things about this deer. Hunting season ended in early December and it would be quite unusual for a hunter to leave a harvested deer lying in the woods. In the right ear of the deer, it was apparent that there was a tag placed, as the loop was there but the tag itself was missing. The strangest thing we noticed was the hide on the neck rolled up over the neck. This is a very uncommon way of field dressing a deer. The team surmised that either the deer was in the process of being dressed and the hunter left quickly, leaving the deer behind, or the deer was brought to the side of the road from another location. Despite our best efforts, we were not able to come up with a rational explanation for the carcass on the side of the road.

The deer carcass was not the only strange thing we found that day. As we were examining the deer, one of the team members noticed what appeared to be a crudely built nest measuring 8 feet deep and 4 feet high. It was intertwined with vines and briars. This possible nest was large enough for one of the investigative team members to crawl inside with room to spare. We wondered if perhaps something brought the deer and placed it next to this possible nest. The research team were only able to make assumptions, as no other evidence was found to support our thoughts, and much like the sightings, the deer and possible nest remain a mystery.

A few interesting side notes about these two sightings. These two January sightings took place within less than a mile of the late July 2009 sighting where the elder sister witnessed a large and small creature. The other interesting side note happened in 2014. When the TV show Finding Bigfoot arrived in town to film the Fayette County episode, Cliff Barackman requested an area where we thought would be ideal for him to camp for his solo camping trip. Because of the number of sightings, we suggested he camp in the woods off of Ferguson Hollow Rd. While camping there, something visited his campsite, and he heard something walking around his tent, and also heard a wood knock. The footage can be seen on the "Paranormal Squatchtivity" episode of Season 7 of Finding Bigfoot.

Before sharing the last case of interest investigated during the flap of 2009 through 2011, I wanted to share a secondhand report shared with our group. Due to his position with the county, the eyewitness refused to be interviewed. The PA Bigfoot Society was not able to investigate this story and only received the information second hand, so we could not validate the encounter. It should be noted that the date and location where it supposedly occurred is during the same area and time where other sightings were being reported. The story and details were told to us by a second hand party who knew the witness and vouched for his credibility. Regardless, I felt it worth sharing as part of the flap of Fayette County.

It was snowing heavily that day in February, 2010, making

visibility and road conditions hazardous. The witness was a county works employee, and he was driving a snow plow that afternoon on Dunbar Creek Road. Dunbar Creek Road is a windy two lane road bordered by Dunbar Creek on the right. The left side of the road is bordered by the forest of Chestnut Ridge. Due to the poor weather and road conditions, the witness was driving at a slow rate of speed plowing snow off to the right side of the road. Even with the windshield wipers on, visibility was very poor.

The driver had just come around a bend in the road and entered a long straight away. In the distance, he saw what he thought was a person wearing dark colored clothes and a dark hooded jacket standing in a snow drift on the left side of the road. Not sure of what the person was going to do and the unsafe road conditions, the man slowed the snow plow down even more.

As the driver approached, the figure walked down from the snow drift and into the roadway on a direct path with the plow. He brought the truck to a complete stop as the figure continued walking right towards his truck, directly in front of the hood. The figure never slowed and without hesitation, stepped over the blade of the snow plow as if it wasn't even there. It continued walking off the roadway in the direction of the creek, down the embankment and out of sight.

The driver shared that from what he could see through his windshield, the figure was dark in color from head to toe. He was not able to make out any clear features, but the head and shoulders were well above the hood of the truck, putting the creature above 7 feet tall. It never once looked in the direction of the driver, and when it stepped over the snow blade of the truck it did so without even slowing down. The witness had the impression that the figure that crossed the road was fearless, and determined to cross the road without letting anything stop it from where it was going. If only the witness would allow us to talk to him in person and share the exact location with the PA Bigfoot Society, we might have been able to search for any clues or evidence that would have validated his story. Unfortunately, it will only remain an interesting story passed along during the Fayette flap of sightings.

During those years, there were numerous encounters, reports of strange screams and sounds, track discoveries and sightings reported to the PA Bigfoot Society. In this section I only covered a handful of the more interesting encounters and sightings we investigated. This last case is one that I felt to be one of the most impressive cases the PA Bigfoot Society members and I ever had the opportunity to investigate during the flap of sightings.

The case involved multiple eyewitnesses over a 3 to 4 week period. Two of the eyewitnesses were law enforcement officers. One of those members was a deputy State Constable at the time, and is now a full Pennsylvania State Constable serving in the Fayette County area. This case also resulted in the Pennsylvania Bigfoot Society capturing some very intriguing audible evidence from the location during the investigation, not to mention the personal experiences had by members of the investigative team. This case is known as the Farmington windmill construction site case, and was featured on the television show Finding Bigfoot.

*Windmill Construction Site, Fairchance, PA
where a security team had repeated encounters in 2011*

In mid-September of 2011, I was contacted by the supervisor of a night time security team hired to guard and watch a windmill construction site in a rural area of the Chestnut Ridge, several miles outside of the small town of Farmington. The windmill construction site was an open site that housed multiple office trailers, storage sheds, buildings, heavy building and construction equipment. The site also served as a secure location for parts and supplies for the windmills being erected along the top of the mountain ridges throughout Fayette County. The location was remote and surrounded by forest and valleys. There were small hunting cabins and a few sparse homes scattered in the area, but scarcely populated.

The security team was hired to monitor and guard the main construction site along with any of the nearby satellite locations to prevent theft or vandalism. The overnight security team was staffed with two men. One would remain at the main site while the other would make random patrols of the satellite locations throughout the night. The supervisor of the security team was a man named Doug. Doug also served as a Deputy State Constable for Fayette County at the time, and is now a State Constable. Doug called me that early September day to share the experiences he and members of his team were experiencing over the course of the past few weeks.

Doug said that over the course of the past 3 to 4 weeks, he and the security crew were experiencing and hearing very strange things at the site. This weird activity was occurring on almost a nightly basis, and beginning to cause a concern to his crew and himself. He stated how he and several other security guards on duty would hear strange sounds emanating from the forests and valleys surrounding the site. Doug and his crew were hearing howls, loud guttural grunts and growling. They would hear high pitched screams, and rhythmic wood knocking sounds that would occur from time to time throughout the night. These sounds would often be accompanied by smells of dead or decaying animals, or very foul odors that would appear on the breeze and then vanish when the sounds subsided.

Doug said his employees had unseen animals approach parked, occupied vehicles, screaming at them before retreating into the forest. One of his employees had a strange occurrence happen while occupying a field toilet early one morning. The guard saw a large human-like shadow pass outside, then a few moments later, something smacked the side of the toilet. After the event occurred, the guard checked in with his coworker on duty, thinking he'd perhaps been messing with him, only to discover his coworker wasn't at the site, but out patrolling the other satellite locations. Doug also shared other strange experiences he and the group had. Eventually Doug went to management of the construction site about the ongoing nightly activity. Management blew him off and told him it was a case of an overactive imagination.

On September 9, Doug found out what he felt was the source of all the strange sounds he and his security guard crew had been hearing. The time was around 3:30 in the morning on September 9th. That night had been quiet and uneventful. Doug was sitting in his parked truck, monitoring the construction site. His truck was parked on a slight rise in the lot, approximately 75 yards from the road and the nearest light pole. The light pole was anchored about 10 feet from the two lane road. On the light pole about four feet up was a large sheet of plywood with several power supply amplifiers and meters attached to it. These fed power to the various trailers, offices and sheds. The light pole was clearly visible from his truck and the light gave off a radius of about 10 feet.

While sitting in his truck, Doug thought he saw movement near the pole. It appeared to him that a large animal on all fours was moving close along the ground toward the light pole. As he watched the animal, it moved up behind the pole and then proceeded to rise up on two legs. The figure then began to play a game of peek-a-boo from behind the power supply board. It would lean out and peer around the far end of the board, looking at Doug before slowly moving back out of sight. This occurred several times as Doug watched. Every time the figure leaned out from the light pole, Doug could see clearly that whatever this creature was, it was not a bear, but looked more like a large hairy person.

This game of peek-a-boo lasted for several minutes before the creature finally stepped back behind the board for the final time. Doug watched as the creature turned and walked away on two legs vanishing into the darkness. After several weeks of wondering what was making all those strange screams, grunts, growls and knocks from the surrounding forests, Doug felt he finally had his answer.

As luck would have it, the PA Bigfoot Society had scheduled a group expedition to Fayette County that very weekend to hike, search and explore areas where sightings and encounters were reported. The timing of Doug's sighting worked out perfectly, as we were able to secure permission from the owners of the construction site and from Doug to allow the group to visit the location and conduct a full investigation. On September 11, the first half of the expedition team arrived in Fayette County.

Expedition members spent the day hiking marked and unmarked trails in the forest surrounding the windmill construction site. The members were split into two teams to cover more ground. Plenty of wildlife and natural forest sign was observed. Neither team experienced or discovered anything unusual or out of the ordinary that would help to validate the claims Doug and the other members of the security team shared with us. We searched the roadway and area near the light pole for tracks but did not find anything left behind.

After our afternoon hike and search of the area, the group broke for dinner with plans to return and meet with Doug for the first of a two night investigation. The team arrived shortly after dark. We met with Doug and two members of the security crew scheduled to work that night. Doug walked us through his sighting of September 9th, and showed us where he saw the creature just days before. The other security guards pointed out locations in the forest where they had heard the strange sounds. They also shared a few of their own personal experiences they had during the past few weeks. In my opinion, eyewitness interviews are best done in person. The person conducting the interview can see the body language, hear the voice inflection, and read the body language displayed when the witness shares their encounter. A face to face interview can be far more telling than an interview conducted over the phone or by email. This was the case when we talked to Doug and the guards that night. We could see that their experiences had them genuinely concerned and nervous. They looked very apprehensive about being at the site and sharing their experiences. It was a good indicator to us that they had experienced something that had a profound impact on them.

The expedition team was very impressed with the witnesses credibility and sincerity when they shared their experiences. We were convinced without a doubt that Doug and the other men we interviewed experienced something unfamiliar to them, and left a lasting impression. We also found no reason for the men to risk their reputations and positions in the law enforcement community by sharing their extraordinary experiences.

During our two night investigation, expedition team members were also witness to many of the strange sounds and noises Doug and his crew shared with us, plus personal encounters that Doug and his team did not experience. Team members reported hearing high pitched screams and low bellowing moans that came from the hills and valleys surrounding the construction site. Group members reported hearing grunts, growls, and wood knocks. I personally heard heavy bipedal foot falls just inside the tree line, and saw eye shine at a very high level moving between the trees. At one point during the night something angrily growled at me when I approached the sounds of footfalls inside the tree line. Members of the expedition team were successful in recording several of these screams and moans during the investigation. These audible sounds can be heard on the audio page of the PA Bigfoot Society at www.pabigfootsociety.com.

At the end of our weekend expedition the team left convinced there was definitely something odd occurring. Over the course of the next several weeks, our team returned to the site multiple times to continue to investigate. During that time, team members recorded and documented other strange sounds, but nothing quite like our first two nights. Our research ended in late October when Doug notified me the site was being closed, the security guard team no longer needed, and the area was considered to be off limits. Members of the PA Bigfoot Society did return to the area from time to time, but no further activity was recorded like it was during the fall of 2011.

As the Fall of 2011 turned to Winter, the activity and sightings seemed to come to an end. Reports still occur in the area but not in the same frequency they did during those two years. It seemed the Fayette flap of sightings had come to an end. Word quickly spread about the flap of sightings and soon Fayette County became a well known hot spot for researchers, investigators and curiosity seekers.

During the summer of 2014, the cast and crew from Finding Bigfoot returned to Pennsylvania. Due to the high number of sightings and activity reported during the flap, Fayette County was chosen as the location to film the second episode known as "Paranormal Squatchtivity." The town hall meeting filmed at the State Hall in Uniontown attracted the largest crowd in Finding Bigfoot history. The episode included many of the witnesses and cases from 2009 to 2011. In January 2015, the episode aired and received positive feedback from the public, other Bigfoot researchers and Bigfoot enthusiasts.

One can look back on the Fayette County flap with wonder and amazement. Many have tried to explain the subsequent increase and decrease of sightings that occurred. Some blame the *Herald Standard* newspaper article of August 2009 as the catalyst for so many reports being filed during that three year period. Others say the flap was sparked by the initial sighting report of July 10, 2009 that opened the flood gates of reports. There were researchers who questioned if perhaps the creatures behavior was simply bolder during that time, allowing themselves to be seen more often. Were the creatures simply allowing themselves to be more visible during those years by moving around more often? Could it just have been a case of good luck? The witnesses being in the right place, at the right time, seeing what they did and then reporting what they encountered? Unfortunately, the truth may never be known as to what started and ended this rash of southwestern Pennsylvania sightings, but mysteries still abound all along the Chestnut Ridge.

Texas Goat Man
by Jeff Stewart

For just about as far back as anyone can remember there have been legends of upright walking man beasts of one kind or another. Today, we have Bigfoot, The Beast of Boggy Creek, Yeti, Skunk Ape, Dog Man, The Lizard Man and the Lake Worth Monster to name a few. But there have always been a few tales that even the most diehard believers of Sasquatch lore shake their heads at. Those creatures who have been coined as "Goat Men" have caused researchers such as myself to scratch our heads in wonder. Here in deep East Texas, we have our own group of things that go bump in the night and skulk around in the swamps and pine thickets. One of which is the Sabine Thing, and the other is the Goat Man.

July of 1969 saw the first of many reported sightings of the Lake Worth Monster. The first officially reported "Goat Man" in Texas of the monster variety. Said to be 7 feet tall and half man, half goat, but also covered in scales. A newspaper article by Terry Deckard titled "Fishy Man Goat Terrifies Couples at Lake," brought the goat man to the public eye. There were many sightings around Lake Worth including one by Tommy Burson, where he reported that a Goat Man creature jumped on the hood of his car out of a tree leaving an almost 2-foot-long gash down the side of the vehicle. It was only after this encounter that local police took any of it seriously. There were reports of the Goat Man of Lake Worth throwing old tires at kids enjoying a party near the lake shore which was witnessed by at least 10 people. The only known photo of the Lake Worth Monster was taken by Allen

Plaster in October of 1969, supposedly during the incident where the tire had been thrown at the kids at the party.

While this may have been the first reported or recognized sighting of the Goat Man. The legendary half goat, half man has been around since the days of Mount Olympus and the Greek and Roman Gods. The Satyr was half goat, half man, the Ithyphallic male consort of the God, Dionysus. These creatures possessed a goat-like head and face and were overly sexual in nature. They were portrayed, in later art work, as having a goat legs and hooves, but originally they were shown with only a goat-like head and face. The chest and shoulders were covered with thick fur. Another subspecies was the Island Satyr. They were reported to be vicious and very violent in nature with long red fur. The Faun was another half goat half man creature found in Roman mythology. The roman God Faunus was himself a goat man. The Faun was believed to play tricks on travelers in certain areas, and help guide the lost. Pan was the Greek God counterpart to Faunus and depicted also as a half man, half goat.

Many cultures and religions have similar legends and beasts in their lore which date back many hundreds and even thousands of years. The half goat, half human creature is nothing new. Even Satan, the Lord of Darkness himself has been depicted for at least a couple of thousand years as having a very goat-like appearance, consisting of horns and hooves in the least, while other characterizations of Satan are almost completely that of a goat, with minimal human traits other than walking upright and having hands. Everywhere we look throughout the histories and mythos of man we find the goat man in some manifestation or another.

Now, there is another Goat Man legend here in Texas which has a bit of a different flare, and an even more horrific human tragedy behind it. There is a bridge in the town of Denton, TX called the Old Alton Bridge. The bridge is about 5 miles out of town and once joined Lewisville to Alton and was constructed around the year 1884. There was a man named Oscar Washburn, who was also known as the Goat Man because he raised and sold goats. Mr. Washburn and his family lived a short distance from the bridge around 1938. Washburn had a reputation as an honest, hard working man with an impeccable character.

Mr. Washburn only had one flaw as seen by certain local lowlifes. Mr. Washburn happened to be African American. A sign at the head of the bridge said "THIS WAY TO THE GOATMANS." For some reason this sign aggravated and enraged the local Klansmen.

On a dark and moonless night in August of 1938 the Goat Man was dragged from his home by the Klan, his hands tied behind his back, a rope tied around his neck and he was savagely hung from the side of the Alton Bridge. When one of the men went to look upon his vile handiwork, he peered over the bridge railing expecting to see the Goat Man hanging there, but all he saw was an empty rope. Thinking he had escaped them the Klansmen returned to the Washburn home where they proceeded to brutalize and murder his entire family.

No one knew if indeed the Goat Man had escaped the Klansmen's murderous grip somehow, or if it was something more supernatural that took hold of him. Since then, there have been many strange sightings on and around the old Alton Bridge which is now referred to as Goat Man Bridge. Many strange happenings, sightings, and disappearances occur around the bridge. Some report seeing a raggedy old man herding goats on or near the bridge. Others report seeing a massive half man, half goat creature carrying a decapitated goat head in his hands. Locals tell this tale of warning to all. If you cross the bridge at night with no headlights on you will be met on the other side by the Goat Man.

There were so many strange things associated with this bridge that a new bridge was constructed beside the old one, but since the old bridge was a historical marker it was left standing and is still open. It is said you can go to the bridge late at night, and if you listen closely you can still hear the sound of goat hooves walking across the bridge. I know this isn't the typical Goat Man creature story, but it fits right in with showing how the Goat Man legends of Texas are many and diverse in nature.

Over the past 30 years I have investigated many strange reports of everything from demon dogs to Bigfoot, but in all of those reports I have had just a few Goat Man reports here in East Texas. What follows are some of them.

On or around October 10th 2006, I got a call from a fellow who was a bit shaken up to say the least. The tale he was spinning seemed wild even to a guy who had been investigating and studying the Bigfoot phenomena and sightings for years. From here on out I will refer to the man reporting this sighting as Mr. R. as he does not want his name used.

Mr. R reported that he had been squirrel hunting along the back side of Lake Murvaul in Panola County when he noticed that nothing was moving. No birds, no squirrels, not even the insects were making any noise. It was, for lack of a better word, DEAD. He crept along as easy and quiet as possible. It soon became evident that for every step he took he could hear an equal yet opposite step almost mirroring his, just out of his sight radius. Thinking it was only an echo he kept slipping along. He soon came to a creek which he had to cross by climbing down one embankment and up the other side. While in the bottom of the creek, he noticed what he first thought was another hunter because it was walking on two legs. As he watched the figure, he was just about to yell out to him for safety reasons, when the figure took what he described as "one hell of a leap," and in one stride made it across the creek, which had to be at least 18 to 20 feet across. Mr. R quickly scaled the opposing embankment. When he reached the top he stood up looking for the guy that had just made an Olympic long jump across the creek without even a running start.

As his eyes scanned the surrounding woods he saw something peer out from behind a huge Overcup Oak tree less than 20 yards away. He could see its features clearly. The creature had the face of what he could only say looked like a man, but not a man. As much like a man as all those old movies made a wolfman resemble a man. The most peculiar thing was he said it looked like it had horns on its head... Horns. It had two small things that appeared to be horns right above where the ears should have been but the whole head was covered in a thick, matted nest of hair, so he wasn't 100% sure they were horns, but to him they sure looked like the horns of a "Nanny goat." The two stared back and forth at one another for what he described as "a month of Sundays." This stare down went on until the creature stepped completely out from behind the tree. Once unobstructed by the tree, Mr. R could see the whole thing. He gave a very strong and detailed description of the beast. He said it stood nearly 7 feet and had to weigh in at around 275 pounds or so, with long arms, and looked nasty, as if it had been sleeping in a pile of leaves, because they were stuck to the dark, reddish, brown hair all over it. He couldn't see any clothes or anything which would make him think it was a man, other than the fact it was walking on two legs and stood upright.

Mr. R went on to tell me that he watched, half frozen with fear and the other half full of curiosity and disbelief, as the creature before him turned its nose slightly upward and to the side and started to sniff the air, as if testing to see if he smelled like something it wanted to eat. At this point he could see the face of the creature from the side. He said it had a wide flat face but not dished in. It had enough hair on its face to hide the jaw and neck but the cheeks and other parts were pretty well bare but looked very dirty. After the creature sniffed the air it turned and took 4 or 5 extremely long strides and was out of sight.

Mr. R told me that he was armed with a 12 gauge shotgun but only had squirrel shot and knew it wouldn't do anything but "PISS OFF" anything that big. Once the creature was gone, and Mr. R had composed himself, he high-tailed it back to his truck and drove straight home. He went in and sat in his recliner trying to decide if he should or could tell anyone. He decided he could not say anything, because everyone would think him a nut job or accuse him of being drunk. Then one day he saw me on social media and knew he could tell me all about it.

As a researcher I find credibility in folks who want no publicity or even recognition for their sighting stories. It lends a certain honesty to their motives for coming forward. Why would anyone with motives less than laudable want no recognition whatsoever? The thing that struck me odd out of all of this was the fact he said it had what looked like horns on its head. Horns? Until now not one sighting I had been told or read about in Deep East Texas involved a creature with Horns. Mr. R had mentioned a few times the Horns looked like little Nanny goat horns. So at the top of the report I had scribbled "GOAT MAN"...

Being that his encounter was on the private property of a hunting club, I couldn't gain access without betraying his confidence, so I never got the chance to do any actual investigating on the property. The report seemed legitimate, and Mr. R was sincere and did not come off as being someone given to flights of fancy. We conversed for quite some time and my conclusion is he truly believed he saw what he claims to have seen.

About a year and a half later I got a message from a lady who claimed to have seen a very similar looking creature while driving down an oil-topped road in Nacogdoches County around Lake Nacogdoches. She reported that while driving home one evening, she and her husband had watched a tall, heavyset creature walk across the road in front of their car. She said they both yelled out "Bigfoot," because at first it looked like all the stuff you see on T.V. — until it turned and looked at them just before it entered the wood line. That's when they saw what looked to be "horns like a goat" on its head above its ears, just like the creature described by Mr. R. This got me to thinking maybe Mr. R had not been mistaken when he thought he saw horns. This second report didn't have much detail and was a very short encounter of only 15 to 30 seconds at most, but they were sure the "Bigfoot" they saw had horns. Now I had heard the tales of the Lake Worth Monster and that they claimed it had horns. Honestly, I had dismissed it as someone simply misidentifying tufts of hair that might have just grown strangely on its head. Just as I had somewhat thought about the supposed horns on Mr. R.'s sighting, but now I had to seriously rethink my previous assessment on what the horn-like protrusions might have been. I now had two reports in a relatively short time frame, from about 50 miles apart and as with the Lake Worth sightings these were coming from near bodies of water. What could it be? What is the Key to these sightings of horned Bigfoot type creatures around bodies of water? Many years went by without any reports, then in 2013 I received a social media message from a guy who claimed to live down around Gary TX. which just happens to be the town closest to Lake Murval. The very lake where the first sighting had occurred.

    As with Mr. R., this gentleman does not want his name used, as he is a Pastor in a local church, and feared it would cost him his position and standing in the community if he went public with what he saw. Which is understandable considering his occupation. A Preacher might find himself without a flock if he started spinning yarns about hairy goat men roaming the woods of East Texas. I guess it's perfectly acceptable to believe in angels, demons and harlots riding dragons, but not a Goat Man or Bigfoot. Now, I mean no disrespect to anyone's religious beliefs. I merely use the reference to point out that what seems irrational and illogical to one may seem totally the reverse to another.

    It seems that during the archery deer season of 2013, while seated in a tree climber deer stand, the Preacher witnessed what was most assuredly the strangest, most unbelievable sight he had ever dreamed of seeing. As daylight broke over a rather warm October morning, the sound of a twig snapping in the distance and leaves rustling got his attention. Looking intently in the direction of the sound, he could make out a large dark figure headed his way on all fours so he figured it was a hog. As he watched it make its way from 100 yards or so out to 50 or 60, at which time he could see it was no hog. While it was out at the 60 yard mark, it did the unbelievable and stood erect on two legs and continued to walk on just two legs. The closer it got, the more detail he could make out. In his words "it had to be a man" because nothing else walked like that on two legs, but it was covered with hair and it had no clothes on. "It had to be a joke." He couldn't be seeing this. He then turned his thoughts to his faith and considered he was witnessing a demon in the flesh, and he closed his eyes for a few seconds to pray. He opened his eyes and it was still there. This time, it had made it a few yards closer as it seemed to be interested in an area where several hogs had been rooting in the dirt. His demon radar really went berserk when he said he noticed it had horns sticking out of his head. He watched and watched for what seemed several minutes. The creature suddenly noticed him sitting in the tree and took off running. At first on two legs, then went down to all fours before going out of sight. He immediately climbed down and left the area.

The Pastor told me that he struggled with what he saw for some time, and even spoke with another member of the clergy who recommended that he tell no one. In the end he decided to talk to me. Knowing me through social media he knew that not only was I a Cryptozoologist but also an ordained Minister and educated at Baptist Christian University. He knew I, above all, could and would look at his experience with a unique set of eyes. After assuring him he had not witnessed some demonic entity risen from the fires of Hell, we came to discuss his sighting quite often, and the one thing he was never wavering on was the fact that the creature he saw had horns. Two small horns jutting up out of his head similar to those of a spike Whitetail buck.

So once again, I had a report of what would be a typical Bigfoot sighting in East Texas if it were not for the horns. Wrapping my head around this wouldn't seem like a monumental task since I already was a Bigfoot investigator with two face to face encounters. But the whole horns thing just posed a question in my mind that I just couldn't come to terms with. Are we dealing with a species of Bigfoot who actually have horns? Are we dealing with a totally separate animal all together not even related to Bigfoot? Or maybe could it really be some sort of demonic hell beast?

Most recently I had a report from a young lady who did not mind having her name used. Mrs. Jodi Fountain reported that she and her sister in law, Mrs. Brandi Fountain, had been sharing a campfire with some friends when they were teens, when they heard something in the bushes behind them. Thinking it was most likely an animal of some kind, they moved cautiously to the other side of the fire. Suddenly a humanoid creature bolted out of the dark as they ran for their cars and left as fast as they could. All that could be said for a description fit exactly what I had heard several times before. Goat Man. It seems Hills Lake road had its own Goat Man. I know their story wasn't a great exciting tale, but not all sightings are super exciting and filled with details. The point is to determine if the sighting is credible or just a bunch of hot air.

You see, East Texas is full of legends, lore and some real live unexplainable things. I have spent the most part of two decades investigating those things everyone else scoffs at. I have been face to face with an upright walking, hair-covered creature twice in my life so far, and had many other encounters that were not quite as up close and personal. But by far, my investigations into the Goat Man of East Texas has had to be about the strangest.

Where do these horns come from? What are they? Again these questions run through my mind over and over. Could the Bigfoot who live around these lakes have adapted, wearing the horns of animals they have killed as a sort of head dress just as other native tribes have for centuries? Is this possible? Why not? These creatures obviously possess an ability for higher thinking, as they have eluded evidentiary scientific substantiation for centuries. Almost every North American native tribe used some sort of animal-themed head dress in one way or another, or could it be something totally different? Could it be these were in fact horns that somehow have grown due to some evolutionary sidetrack or even a necessity? The fact remains that report after report comes in telling of Bigfoot type creatures with horns.

I have as yet not seen one of these creatures with the horns, but have witnessed Bigfoot creatures on two separate occasions with mud so caked in their hair that it hung in long, thick clumps almost akin to dreadlocks. Had these been dry and on the head one might have mistaken them for horns at a medium distance. Is this a possible answer? Of course it is but so is just about everything else. The realm of possibilities is not limited by what we know only what we don't.

In the Mountains of Nevada

Silver State Sasquatch

By David Weatherly

The dusty landscape of Northern Nevada shimmered in the afternoon heat as my jeep left the pavement and hit dirt road. We were almost a hundred miles from Reno off Interstate 80, winding down after a week and a half of exploring mysteries across the Silver State. Riding shotgun was my friend and fellow investigator, Dave Spinks.

Dust Devils in the Nevada Desert

We followed the rough dirt track about twenty miles out from the nearest town. Finally, the trail curved to the left and started a slow climb. At the top was a small parking area and a worn historic sign. Climbing out of the jeep we took in the surroundings, a vast view of stark, dry mountains and desert landscape. In the distance, a dust devil kicked up and we watched as it moved to the west and faded away. To our right, a rocky outcropping stabbed into the blue sky. A brief hike up the trail would wind up and around in a circle, taking us to the other side of the mountain and the opening that we sought. The entrance to a historic location connected to a Paiute legend of red haired giants that some believed were the creatures we now call Sasquatch. We were standing at the base of the famous Lovelock Cave.

Nevada, the Silver State.

Mention Nevada and people usually think of two things; hot, dry deserts, and Las Vegas, the city of lights, or, as it's otherwise known, sin city. Vegas is a tourist mecca and one of the world's top gambling destinations, but its fame and glitter often overshadow the rest of what the state has to offer.

Nevada is the 7th largest state in the union. At 110,567 square miles, it's roughly the size of Italy. It has ten deserts and is in fact the driest state in the US, but there's much more to the state. Few people realize how diverse Nevada really is. Beyond its deserts, there are lush forests, mountains and valleys. The state has several hundred mountain ranges. Its highest point, Boundary Peak, reaches 13,140 feet and over thirty other peaks pass the 11,000-foot mark. It's the most mountainous U.S. state in the contiguous 48. Some of the major named ranges include the Battle, Ruby, Sierra Nevada, Snake and Toiyabe ranges.

Nevada's ecosystems are diverse and it has six different biotic zones: alpine, sub-alpine, ponderosa pine, pinion-juniper, sagebrush and creosote bush.

It's rated the 9th least densely populated state in the union. Nearly three quarters of its citizens live in Clark County which contains the Las Vegas-Paradise metropolitan area, where three of the state's four largest incorporated cities are located.

Beyond the tourist sights of Las Vegas lie the sweeping deserts and high mountain forests. Much of the land is uninhabited, speckled with caves, abandoned mines and mine shafts. Populations are sparse in small towns around the state and ghost towns abound, leftover attempts at settlement from the heyday of mining. The state remains one of the world's largest producers of gold and also produces a large amount of silver.

The Southern third of Nevada is within the Mojave Desert and the low terrain experiences hot summer days and chilly to cold winter nights as the result of temperature inversion. In the north, winters can be long and cold with ample snowfall. With such vast, uninhabited areas, and a wealth of resources including food and water, the potential for an undiscovered creature to hide out in the wilds of the Silver State are high. I've personally taken many excursions across Nevada and there are countless intriguing stories to be found among the rural areas.

The Path to Lovelock Cave

During our trek across Northern Nevada, Dave and I had spent some time at Pyramid Lake on the Paiute Reservation outside of Reno. We were digging into the legend of "water babies" (an intriguing tale for another time), and decided to make a stop at the Paiute tribe's official visitor center on the road to the lake.

Pulling up in the parking lot, I made a comment to Dave about an odd looking sculpture sitting in an enclosed area at the back of the center.

Legend of the Red Haired Giants

"That looks like a Sasquatch," I noted.

"Yeah kinda, but why would they have that here?" Dave replied.

We didn't stop to focus on the statue then, choosing instead to go inside and check out the center. In the building were various artifacts from the Paiute tribe and plenty of information about the tribe's history and the history of Pyramid Lake itself. But we were interested in more than just the usual fare of historical tidbits and general interest. I wanted to see if we could learn more about the Paiute legend of the "water babies," strange creatures said to lurk deep in Pyramid Lake. Since such tales are a part of tribal lore, we spent some time talking with tribal members at the center and gathered some more general information. We were very fortunate to have a tribal elder take some of his time and fill us in on the water baby legend, providing some interesting leads to pursue down by the waterside.

As we left the center, I again spotted the statue out back and had to take a better look. On close examination, it was clear that the sculpture, made from reclaimed barbed wire, was a depiction of a Sasquatch adult standing alongside a juvenile version of the creature.

It was too compelling to ignore so we went back into the center in time to catch the elder we had spoken with. He told us the sculpture was made by a local artist who collected pieces of barbed wire in the desert and wove them together. The statue was a representation of the creatures the tribe called "Si-Te-Cah."

The elder began to spin the tale of the Si-Te-Cah. It was a story I'd heard before, but never directly from a tribal member. We listened intently as his words transported us back in time:

"Long ago, this region was lush and rich with wild game, plants and water. There was a great river that flowed in the basin. Fish were abundant and along the banks grew many plants that the tribe ate and used for healing and other purposes. Life was very good, at least mostly good. But there was something the tribe feared. Up in the hills around the river lived the Si-Te-Cah. They were giants with red hair and they preyed on the tribe. They were cannibals.

They hunted members of the tribe for food. The Si-Te-Cah carried woven baskets on their backs. These baskets had spikes all around that pointed down into the basket. They would catch a person and shove them into the basket and the person couldn't get away because the spikes would stab them if they tried. They would carry their victims up into the mountains and eat them. They were terrible creatures.

Discovering Statues of the Si-Te-Cah

The Paiutes were not the only tribe that suffered the attacks of the Si-Te-Cah, the cannibals would prey on all the natives in the region. Finally, the various tribes gathered and had a meeting. They decided they would band together and put a stop to the terror of the giants in the mountains.

A great band of warriors set out after the giants. They pursued the Si-Te-Cah up into the hills and chased them into a cave there. They shouted and demanded that the giants come out and face them in battle, but the Si-Te-Cah refused. They stayed inside the cave.

The warriors gathered brush and wood and piled it up high around the entrance of the cave. Again, they called out to the giants and told them to come out and face them in battle like warriors, but the Si-Te-Cah would not come out of the cave. The warriors gave them a final chance to come out and end the standoff with honor in combat, but the giants would not listen so the warriors set fire to the brush. The fire burned big and strong, filling the cave and burning everything inside. The Si-Te-Cah were burned alive and the terror of the cannibal giants was put to an end.

Lovelock Cave

The cave is still there to this day. The inside is black and you can still see the soot on the walls from when the giant cannibals were burned alive by the warriors."

When the elder was done with his tale, we stood in silence for a moment. We asked a couple of questions for clarity, then thanked him again for his time. We quietly left the center, stopping to take another look at the barbed wired sculpture of the Si-Te-Cah before making our way to the lake.

The following day, with the elder's account still fresh in our minds, we found ourselves taking an exit off of Interstate 80 and pulling into the small town of Lovelock.

Lovelock is a dot on the map with a quaint downtown area around a courthouse. A small sign displayed the town's name and as we rode through town, we noted the unusual number of redheads that were walking around the streets. Coincidence perhaps, but notable nonetheless in a small town in Northern Nevada. I parked and we made our way to the local library where we were able to get directions to the legendary cave on the outskirts of town.

And so, we came to find ourselves at the base of Lovelock cave, looking up at the rocks that held the entrance to a legend.

As a footnote, I should mention at this point, that the journey to the cave itself was not without incident as we encountered, in the middle of nowhere, what can only be described as an MIB (Men in Black) type character. As it bears no direct relevance to our examination of Sasquatch in this text, I'll simply say it's a story for another time and place.

The Blackened Walls of Lovelock Cave

Once we were inside the cave, we found conditions to be exactly as the elder had described. The entrance is tucked into jagged rocks and inside there is a wooden platform, built sometime along the way to make it easy for people to go inside and view the interior of the cave. The cave is an archeological site and during excavations a large number of artifacts were removed.

Archeologists insist the Paiutes actively used the cave for many years and attribute the artifacts to them. Tribal authorities insist the Paiutes did NOT use the cave. Historians and scholars insist the Paiutes are misinformed about their own tribal history.

Inside the cave, the walls and ceiling are black, evidence of a massive fire inside long ago. Visitors to the site are rare, and if one was not familiar with the legend of the giants, the cave would simply be a small, archeological site that only those interested in regional history might find notable.

Allegedly, among the artifacts removed from the caves were a pair of sandals that measured fifteen inches. While in today's world, there are plenty of basketball players that wear shoes of such size, the Paiutes of days long past would not have come anywhere close to such a shoe size. It's another puzzling piece of the mystery of Lovelock cave.

Even more fascinating are the rumors of giant skulls retrieved from the cave. According to some claims, in 1967, an ancient skull was found near or in Lovelock cave. It resembled that of a Neanderthal skull and had a protruding brow ridge, sloping forehead and a large occipital bun—all traits rare in modern humans. Purportedly, the skull did not resemble those of American Indians either. Numerous researchers have attempted to locate these mysterious bones, but sadly, the trail to such artifacts has gone cold. We're left to wonder if the stories of the skull are a historical conspiracy, a fabricated tale of pure fancy, or a misinterpretation of facts.

While the legends are fascinating, the obvious question is how much truth is there to the to the whole story of the Si-Te-Cah in general? Were these creatures, these giant cannibals, just a part of the spiritual belief system of the tribe? Were they pure mythology? Or is there something more to it? The Paiutes are adamant about their tale of the Si-Te-Cah and the fact that it's not just folklore, but a valid account from the tribe's history. An account of a physical battle that took place. There's certainly the cold, hard fact that the cave exists and contains evidence of a massive fire having burned inside it at some time in history.

Sarah Winnemucca, a Northern Paiute author, activist and educator, recounted the tale of the battle with the Si-Te-Cah in her book, "Life Among the Piutes: Their Wrongs and Claims," published in 1883. The book is both a memoir and a history of the tribe during its first forty years of contact with Europeans.

At one time, the cave may have gone deeper into the mountains or even underground, but if such an entrance exists, it is long covered over or hidden. If Lovelock has more secrets, it's keeping them. At least for now.

Modern Monsters

Ancient native accounts aren't the only evidence of hairy beasts roaming around Nevada. While the number of modern reports is fairly small overall, it's important to remember the remote areas of the state where these creatures are likely to exist are also sparsely populated regions. Additionally, a lot of people in such rural areas are reluctant to discuss their strange encounters openly.

The BFRO (Bigfoot Field Researcher's Organization) maintains a Website for reports of Sasquatch filed by state. The site's report section for Nevada has a series of interesting reports from a man who grew up in Northwestern Nevada. There's a total of three reports from the same witness, relating events that took place in Washoe County in the area outside of Reno in the 1970s. This of course was a time when the population of Reno was much, much smaller and urban sprawl was quite limited.

The witness's father was a geologist and preferred to live in sparsely populated areas. Growing up, the man spent ample time in the outdoors camping, hunting for rocks and artifacts, and panning for gold in the hills. His early encounters came when he was a boy. Bigfoot was not a common topic of conversation in the 1970s so the young man didn't have solid points of reference for the creature until later in life.

In the man's third and most interesting account, he talks about his family moving into one of the first "new developments" on the east side of Lemmon Valley outside of Reno. It was when the family first moved to their new home that the young man had his most startling encounter with a large, bipedal creature that was being pursued by a pack of feral dogs.

Late one night, the witness was up reading when he heard the pack of wild dogs clearly in pursuit and attack mode. The animals were getting closer and closer to his house and he assumed they were on the trail of another animal and were moving in for the kill. As the pack drew near, whatever the dogs were chasing suddenly rushed into the back yard of the young man's home. He listened closely to the sounds, and as he recounts:

"For just a second, I could hear it running, as the sound of the dogs was still partially masked around the corner of the garage. As it covered the twenty feet between the two corners, I head three distinct, heavy footfalls ... This was followed by an incredible impact into the corner of the house. The force was so great that I could hear the four-by-four upright in the wall crack and the whole room shook. The impact and cracking sound came from a point about five and a half feet above the level of the ground outside. Simultaneously, there was a secondary impact about seven feet above ground level across the top right corner of my window as viewed from outside. The window rattled violently in the frame and I was sure it was cracked. Immediately following the two simultaneous impacts, there was a forced grunt as if the wind had been knocked out of whatever it was and I could hear its body fall heavily to the ground.

My first thought was, "Oh my God!! They're chasing a man!" The footfalls were clearly bipedal, the height of the impacts was too high for it to be anything four-legged, and the sound of it having its wind knocked out was manlike, if somewhat heavy."

The witness noticed the "man" never cried out for help or made any other vocal noises as one would expect in such a situation. Thinking he had to do something to assist, the witness headed for his window, intending to open the drapes and yell out at the dogs. As he was moving to do just this, he received another surprise:

"...it didn't sound like the dogs were mauling the man. They were about three feet from the house, stationary, barking and growling. It sounded as if there were only three of them, two very aggressive and ready to attack, and one that was barking the way a dog would if it were afraid of you, but ready to attack if provoked.

Just as my fingertips touched the drapes, the scariest thing I have ever experienced in my life happened (believe me, this is saying a lot for someone who has spent nineteen years in the military and lived through a parachute malfunction.) Somehow the man had recovered from hitting the house, having the wind knocked out of him, and falling. He had somehow managed to stand up and get his breath back and just as I touched the drapes, from a point immediately outside my window, level with and about two feet from my head, he growled back at the dogs.

The growl wasn't loud. It was only about two and a half seconds long. But it was the meanest, deepest, and most menacing growl I have ever heard in my life. (To include those of trapped brown bears at Yellowstone.) It was almost as if he was keenly aware that there were people around, that he knew precisely how long he had to growl to get his point across, and that he didn't want to make any more noise than he absolutely had to."

Several seconds of dead silence followed until the creature brushed back by the corner of the house and headed for a six-foot cedar fence at the back of the property. The creature cleared the fence and the dogs momentarily barked and jumped against the fence in frustration before rounding the corner and taking up the trail again. The witness listened as the sound of the dogs, back in pursuit, faded into the distance.

After that night, the pack of feral dogs, that had been plaguing the neighborhood since the houses were built, was never seen or heard of again."

These reports are revealing as they come from a time before the legend of Bigfoot was spread around the world via documentaries and reality television. The accounts are well written and more lengthy and detailed than is common.

BFRO investigator Dr. Wolf H. Fahrenbach made a statement regarding the reliability of the witness:

"The witness is eminently credible and imbues his reports with admirable environmental descriptive detail. Details of the encounter are such that they leave no alternative other than a sasquatch."

A Beast Near Winnemucca

The BFRO website also records an account from Humboldt County near the town of Winnemucca in the Northern Central portion of the state. According to the account, the witness, along with an uncle and six-year-old cousin, were exploring the mountains surrounding Winnemucca, and were walking up the foot of a mountain on the ridge of a wash. It was February, 2005 and there was about a foot and a half of snow on the ground. According to her account:

"...my cousin said that she saw a guy standing on top of the mountain and I said "There's no one up there, it's too far from any civilization. It's probably just a juniper bush." But about five minutes later, our 95 pound Doberman/Greyhound mix made a mad dash underneath the truck by the foot of the mountain. (And our dog was not one to be scared off easily, its scares away anything that comes close to the house, and it even took on a mountain lion once, it has the scars on its underbelly to prove it.) Just about the time me and my uncle looked up towards where my cousin was pointing, we heard a low, droning howl and what I thought was the juniper bush, was animated now, walking downwards, and swaying side to side slightly. It spooked me and my uncle because on the way up we saw a totally decimated cow carcass! About that time we headed out to the truck because we were pretty shaken up by what we had just seen. We were reluctant to tell anyone in fear of being laughed at and ridiculed."

The witness said this sighting took place about an hour and a half before sunset and that conditions were clear.

BFRO investigator John Salmond followed up on the report and found the witness credible. He was told the group observed the figure for about five minutes. The witness further stated that the figure was all black and that no neck was visible, rather, the head seemed to slope down into the shoulders.

Encounters in the Pine Nut Mountains

The Pine Nut Mountains are a north-south range located in the Great Basin of northwestern Nevada. As the name implies, the mountains are rich in Pinyon pine trees whose nuts have long been a dietary staple of the Washoe tribe. The highest peak is Mount Siegel which rises to 9,456 feet. Carson City is about an hour's drive from the mountains.

There are numerous springs in the area that provide fresh water, ample wildlife, and edible vegetation. It's also another area where a number of people have reported giant, hairy creatures.

On the Bigfoot Encounters Website, there's an account from a member of the Washoe tribe who had a disturbing experience near Minden in the Pine Nut Mountains.

It was October, 1994 when the man turned off highway 395 and journeyed eighteen miles to cut firewood for the coming winter season. Driving down a logging road, he ended up with the transmission line on his vehicle ruptured, and was left with no choice but to walk out of the forest.

It grew dark as he was walking and after trekking eight miles, he encountered something he'd never heard before:

"When I heard the first scream, I was so startled I jumped two feet in the air. I never go in the mountains unarmed. I was carrying a 30 round SKS. I could hear this beast was extremely angry and coming straight at me. I threw the safety off of my rifle and fired 10 rounds overhead where the creature was making his noise, which would have been 50 yards to the south of me.

It stopped its advance towards me. Then it started to move in the opposite direction uphill, all the while screaming and breaking trees along the way until it crested a large hill. I continued to walk to town thinking to myself what would have been the outcome if I had not been armed."

The man was eventually picked up by family members who had been out searching for him. He reported his encounter to tribal authorities but no further follow ups have been reported.

The Jarbidge Monster

Over a hundred miles north of Elko, down long stretches of lonely dirt roads, lies the unincorporated town of Jarbidge. Sitting within the 113,167 acre Jarbidge Wilderness in the mountains of Elko County in northeastern Nevada, it's a remote town not easily accessible. In fact, Jarbidge lays claim to being the most isolated town in the lower 48 states, tucked in amongst rivers and tall mountain peaks.

In this quiet little town you'll find flowing brooks, rivers and alpine lakes. These waters are full of mountain whitefish and Redband trout that draw in fishermen from around the world. There are big game camps that stay busy in the fall and summer months as hunters come in to take advantage of the flourishing populations of Mule deer, Rocky Mountain Elk and other game that roam throughout the Jarbidge Wilderness.

But according to Shoshone legend, there may be something else lurking in the remote mountains and forest.

Tsawhawbitts.

Shoshone legends state that a giant cannibal named Tsawhawbitts (pronounced "tuh-saw-haw-bits") roamed Jarbidge canyon looking for unsuspecting humans. Tribal tales claim the giant would capture humans, toss them in a large basket that it carried on its back, and take them to its camp in the hills where it would consume them. The monster hid in the deep ravines, caves, and lava tubes in the region and ranged from Northern Nevada up into present day Idaho.

If the story sounds startlingly similar to the Paiute tales of the Si-Te-Cah, there could be good reason. The Shoshone, Paiute and Washoe tribes all inhabited the region before European settlers moved in. Because of their proximity, there are obvious connections between the tribes and some tales are similar. However, the story of Tsawhawbitts has some aspects that make it unique from the Si-Te-Cah, and it has come to be tied in directly to the town of Jarbidge in unusual ways.

When Europeans came to the area, they discovered the Shoshone avoided the region because they feared the evil creature. As a result, the area was mostly uninhabited and remained that way until gold was discovered in the hills in the early 1900s. Prospectors flooded in, creating the last great American gold rush. One prospector, Dave Bourne, heard the legend of the giant creature feared by the Shoshone and decided to name the town after it. In some strange way, the mispronunciation of the Shoshone term Tsawhawbitts morphed into "Jahbich" and eventually, Jarbidge.

Even the gold rush only did so much for the small community. The town's population reached its peak in 1911, growing to 1500 people. All major mining operations in the area were suspended by 1941.

In "Legends of Spirit Cave," by Dennis Cassinelli, the author relates the legend of the Shoshone and their struggle with the giant in their homeland, the lush hunting grounds along the Bruneau river. The tale of the hairy beast is told through the voice of the character Bruneau, a tribal storyteller:

"Tsawhawbitts was huge! In one step, he could cross the turbulent Bruneau. In a few fleet strides, he could climb a mountain. No one was safe! On his broad back the giant carried a basket which he filled with our hunters for his own feast. Whenever he became hungry, the giant would pull out one of the men and eat them. From his great height Tsawhawbitts could spy on lone wanderers and swoop down upon them before they could flee. Snatching them up from the river bank or a tall pine thicket, Tsawhawbitts would stuff them in his basket and then disappear into a crater name Mount Ichabod where he made his home."

In this version of the tribe's history, their original land was in what is now Southwestern Idaho, territory still historically associated with them. In Bruneau's tale, the giant drove the tribe away from its best lands:

"First in small numbers, then in a great panic-stricken migration, my people fled in all directions. This is how we came to be here in the marsh country. Gradually, some of us were assimilated by lesser tribes; others continue searching for a suitable homeland to this day. Only I remain here to tell you this tale. I have not heard from my people in all these years since they abandoned me here in this place. With each passing generation, memories of the verdant north country diminish. The great fear we have of Tsawhawbitts, the evil spirit, remains constant as it is told and retold. It must be known that the lush hunting area of Jarbidge and the Bruneau river must be avoided as if there were a plague. Our tribal memory of this evil spirit will be handed down for many generations."

The Jarbidge referred to in this case is the Jarbidge River, located in Idaho. Mount Ichabod however, is Southwest of the town of Jarbidge so it seems that the tale of the giant was spread far and wide by tribal members. While the storyteller calls the monster an "evil spirit," it is important to note the lines become blurry when translating ancient native lore into modern verbiage. What may seem to be mere folklore to modern readers, was taken as literal fact by the original people telling the tales.

Some versions of the story say that Tsawhawbitts was an "evil spirit in superhuman form" implying a much more physical manifestation of the creature. This would make sense when we consider that the Shoshone were likely trying to make sense of something so frightening in their midst.

Tradition says the creatures would often be observed on high, rocky peaks digging in the ground. The Shoshone also believed Tsawhawbitts had supernatural powers, including glowing red eyes that gave them the ability to paralyze their prey. It only took a quick glance from the creature and the victim was trapped, unable to resist or flee, allowing Tsawhawbitts to harpoon the victim with razor sharp claws or hooks.

The legends have held fast in the region and are reflected in place names such as central Idaho's Sawtooth mountains where one can find "Coapiccan Kahni" or the "Giant's House," a peak thought to be one of the dwelling places of the giant cannibals. No one seems to know where the giants got their craving for the taste of human flesh. The deadly creatures often hid in caves deep in the mountains. If such a cave was found, warriors would lie in wait to ensure the giant was inside. Once this was confirmed, they would pile brush and wood at the entrance and light it on fire, throwing more and more fuel on it until the flames reached inside the cave and burned the beast alive. It's possible that this part of the tale was carried over from the Paiute encounter at Lovelock cave and that Shoshone warriors were part of the original war party that encountered the giants there.

Locals still talk about the "Jarbidge Monster," and accounts of strange, hairy creatures still come out of the vast wilderness that surrounds the remote town.

The Jarbidge Ranger District is part of the Humboldt-Toiyabe National Forest, a sprawling, rugged region of 243, 907 acres. There's a wide range of temperatures and vegetation in this part of the state and it's noted as being one of the least used wilderness areas in the United States.

Fresh water is available in the region and it receives an average of 100 inches of snow in the winter. There's subalpine fir and white bark pine at higher elevations, aspen groves along the lower basins, big cottonwoods along the river sides and Rocky Mountain juniper at the lower elevation slopes. Plenty of cover and resources for large creatures to live undetected.

A retired ranger who once worked the region told me:

"Honestly, for years, I never believed in Bigfoot, but I've seen some unsettling things in the Jarbidge wilderness. If such a giant, undiscovered creature lives anywhere, it's in the Jarbidge.

I've talked to some folks who told me some pretty unsettling stories about things they've encountered in the wilderness of Nevada, and I think I'm wise enough at this point to just accept that there are some things out there that we just don't know enough about and don't yet understand."

Modern Encounters in the Jarbidge Mountains

A compelling and frightening modern encounter turned up on the Nevada Sasquatch Website. "Mike C." a resident of Reno, posted a long account detailing his encounters with aggressive creatures while on a hunting trip in the Jarbidge Mountains of northern Elko County. The account was published in May 2015 and titled: "Bigfoot: Hunters Encounter An Aggressive Group of Sasquatch in the Jarbidge Mountains of Northern Nevada."

Mike has purportedly suffered some psychological trauma due to the aggressive nature of his encounters. As with many witnesses, recounting his tale was likely a cathartic exercise and we can only attempt to understand what he went through by reading closely and trying to see through his eyes.

Mike had hunted the Jarbidge area before, and in fact, the trip in question would take him back to the same campsite he had used three years in a row. It was 2014 when Mike packed his gear and sat off to bow hunt Mule Deer in the Jarbidge Mountains. Along on the journey this time was Mike's stepdad who was taking his first hunting trip into the Jarbidge wilderness.

Before their journey started, Mike noted the area was being hit with an unusual amount of rain and more thunderstorms were in the forecast for the coming days. The men planned accordingly, packing rain gear and tarps for the nasty weather. Arriving at the remote, wilderness site, something seemed amiss right from the start. While setting up camp, Mike began to feel very uneasy, as he recounts:

"...I started to feel not right about the situation. I got that nagging feeling of dread and of being watched. The rain had stopped for the last few hours and it was dead silent. In the 3 years I've been there I've never heard it that quiet, It was that deafening quiet."

Mike did his best to shrug off the odd feelings and he and his stepdad continued the process of setting up camp and organizing their gear in preparation for the days to come. The men had no restrictions or timeline in mind and intended to stay until they'd had their fill and/or had taken enough game. They had even arrived a couple of days before the season officially started so they could set up camp and spend some time scouting the area before the hunt.

Mike recalls the first night as he prepared to get some sleep. He'd left his flashlight and sidearm in the vehicle and wasn't comfortable without them due to the wild animals that roamed the region. He made his way to the truck, parked about 10-12 yards from the trailer they'd set their bedding up on and had an experience he'll never forget:

"…right as I was about to open the door, lightning flashed and 6-7 yards in front of me was the silhouetted figure of an upright, standing, two-legged, hairy man with a slight conical shape to the head. It appeared that it was going from right to left and not directly facing me and then it all went black and eerie thunder crackled."

Mike's quick sighting was the first sign that the men would have trouble that night. Retrieving his gun and flashlight, he felt a bit safer and tried to convince himself that the sighting had been his imagination.

Climbing back under the tarp, he settled in and tried to sleep. But the night got much worse. A range of sounds started to issue around the tarp. Footsteps, grunts and growls, things being thrown against the tarp itself. At one point, something grabbed the tarp and pushed down on it. Even the trailer itself was violently shaken.

Mike reported something urinating just outside the tarp, at the end where his head was. He recounts that the volume sounded like that of a horse or large bull. Something, it seemed, was marking its territory.

Whatever was out there was unhappy that the men were present and the displeasure was being made obvious.

Unsure what to do, the two men climbed out of the tarp and headed for the truck. It gave them a chance to take a good look around the camp. The creatures, it seemed, were still present:

"We climb out and there's tracks everywhere, good tracks, bad tracks, tracks with claws coming off the toes. Our firewood is everywhere, and a big chunk was torn off a tree from approximately 11 feet up. To my left is the truck and the thickest brush and trees and I can hear one moving in there. The ones out in front that were throwing rocks started throwing rocks at us and the two that were behind my stepdad had come back up behind the trailer and started shaking it."

Clearly, it was time to leave. Climbing into the truck, the men headed into the nearest town and slept in the cab until the following morning. They decided to go back to the camp in the daylight and retrieve their gear. Making their way to the site, they found it much as it had been the night before at their sudden departure. As they started packing up the camp, Mike spotted a creature nearby watching them:

"...I'm staring at a Sasquatch who is staring straight back at me. It was 8:30am against a cloudless piercing blue sky. It had to of wanted us to see it. It didn't appear to be trying to hide and had purposely sky lined itself."

Mike watched as the creature took off and ran uphill and into a ravine. He describes it as having burnt auburn, cinnamon colored hair that covered everything, with thinner looking hair on the chest and thicker hair on the arms. He said the face had a "wide smashed down looking nose with piercing dark eyes that looked recessed back into the head more than you or me."

Exposed skin was noted as being of lighter color then the hair with a "slightly buckskin kind of coloration." The mouth was wide and the head was conical shaped and came directly out of the shoulders with no visible neck. The man states that height was difficult to judge as the creature appeared to be crouching, but he believes it was at least 7-8 feet and possibly taller.

Mike and his stepdad relocated their camp to a forest service campground 8-10 miles away from the site of the encounters. They hoped the distance, combined with being in an established campground, would cause the creatures to leave them alone. But the encounters continued.

Mike reports that, for the most part, the additional encounters were not as angry and aggressive as the initial contact. Still, the entire experience left him quite rattled and from his writing, he still hasn't completely come to terms with the encounters. There's much more to Mike C's account including details of some of his time at the forest service campground. The full account is well worth a read and is still posted at NevadaSasquatch.blogspot.com.

Battle Mountain

There's another curious tale of Sasquatch in Northern Nevada that received a lot of publicity, at least among the community of Bigfoot researchers and Websites. It involved a supposed incident at a site called Battle Mountain and a strange creature caught in a raging forest fire.

The BFRO originally received the report, a story about a wounded Sasquatch, but later dismissed the claims made by the anonymous witness. According to the original information, the witness was on the scene himself and reports what occurred:

"I observed an animal wounded by fire moving on all fours not like a bear. More like ape. Fire Fighters captured animal, contacted local vet and medical doctor, U.S. Department of Fish and Wildlife, Department of Interior, and Bureau of Land Management on the scene."

The mysterious report goes on to state:

"Animal tranquilized and moved to unknown location. Those at scene told not to talk about what they saw."

The creature was described as seven and a half feet in height. It was suffering from 2nd and 3rd degree burns on its hands, feet, legs and body. So, we have an anonymous government employee, a vast conspiracy of silence imposed on numerous officials, and a body that is quietly taken away to an "undisclosed location." All in all, a very "X-Files" type of account. Area 51 anybody?

All things considered, some might consider the story hardly worth mentioning, but there are a couple of interesting points:

Bigfoot researcher, author and science teacher, Thom Powell took up the case and promoted the story as probably genuine and a likely government coverup. Powell is respected by a lot of people in the field, so it helped the story continue to circulate.

It's also curious to note that Battle Mountain, Nevada lies between Lovelock and the Jarbidge Mountains. The small town lies just off of Interstate 80 in the North central part of the state, a region where the Natives have a history of cornering giant cannibals in the mountains and burning them. Coincidence? Maybe.

Around the State

Nevada sits in an interesting location in terms of the creatures known as Sasquatch, especially if they are migratory as many researchers believe. Bordering California, Oregon and Idaho to the West and North, and Utah and Arizona to the East and South, the creatures may utilize the vast wilderness regions of Northern Nevada as stopping points on their journeys, or as homes and hunting grounds during part of the year.

Tracks have been found in the Diamond Mountains near Eureka in the middle of the state. Prints have been found on numerous occasions close to the Owyhee River Wilderness near the borders of Idaho and Oregon. Scattered reports from people who have trekked some of the region's wilderness speak of large, bipedal creatures lurking in the forests.

The Humboldt National Forest covers around 7,935 square miles. There are few routes through it. The Lake Tahoe region has around 14,000 acres of undeveloped forest. The area is popular with tourists from all over the country, but primarily from California and other parts of Nevada, and news reports have cropped up over the years that mention the creatures in the Tahoe region.

In August 1973, the *Reno Evening Gazette* received a letter from two couples who mentioned a frightening experience on the shore of Lake Tahoe. Driving up Kingsbury Grade on a July evening, they saw what they first assumed was a black bear. When they got closer to the animal, they discovered it standing upright on two legs. They stated that the animal was shiny and about seven feet tall. They described the face as "flat, like a gorilla's."

Eleven years later, two women hiking on the east side of the Sierra Nevadas above Lake Tahoe met two teenage boys who tried to warn them away from the mountain. The boys told the women that if they proceeded any farther up the trail, they would encounter a "monster." The women ignored the boys, thinking it was a joke or utter nonsense. They continued their course, gathering pinecones for a project, when they did indeed encounter a "monster." At first glance, the women thought it was a man in a bear suit. His arms hung nearly to his knees when he walked and a foul odor preceded him. He was seven-foot-tall and covered in fur that the witnesses stated was "the color of dry pine needles."

The women fled the area, and looking back during their retreat, they could still see the creature, crouched on a boulder and staring at them.

Down towards the middle of the state, in the small town of Ely, two friends were riding on a dirt road near Telegraph Summit in 2001 when they had a strange encounter.

The two riders were ten miles off Highway 93 when they stopped to take a break for water. They caught wind of something they described as smelling like "rotten garbage."

Dusk was approaching, and suddenly the rocky, mountainous area around them was ringed with "weird howls." They reported the sounds were like nothing they'd ever heard before. They spent about ten minutes trying to imitate the howls then decided it was best to leave the scene.

As they departed, they spotted a "brownish, ape-like" creature between seven and eight feet in height dashing into the trees.

Nuclear Sasquatch

Perhaps the most unusual Nevada Sasquatch encounter occurred in 1980 at no less than the Nevada Test Site. Now known as the "Nevada National Security Site," the location is a United States Department of Energy reservation in southeastern Nye County, about 65 miles from Las Vegas.

The site is 1,360 square miles of desert and mountain terrain. It was originally established in 1951 for the testing of nuclear devices. Throughout the 1950s, citizens of Las Vegas would frequently see the iconic mushroom clouds that resulted from the one hundred atmospheric tests conducted at the location. The clouds even became a tourist attraction in the days when people had little concern or knowledge about the potential negative effects of nuclear energy and fallout. In total, 928 nuclear tests were conducted at the site, most of them, 828, were underground.

Although the site is no longer used for nuclear testing, it remains a secured site and is actively studied to learn more about the longterm effects of radiation. Public tours are offered but visiting rules are very strict. No cameras, binoculars or cell phones are allowed. Visitors are not permitted to pick up rocks from the site and all areas of the location are monitored by security. No one crosses the borders without a security badge, unless they're accompanied on an official tour.

It was January 1980 when wire services picked up an unusual report from the site. A Bigfoot had been sighted spotted crossing the Tippipha Highway between the site's control point and Area 12 camp, right in the middle of the testing ground. The man who witnessed the creature rushed to the test site's command post at "Mercury" and reported a beast that was "somewhere between six and seven feet tall, standing erect and walking like a man, with dark hair completely covering its body."

It would have remained an unknown incident, except that an employee at the site contacted the *Las Vegas Sun* and let the story out. The site's public information officer at the time, Dave Jackson, was suddenly busy fielding calls. He recalls the incident:

"I called and got ahold of security, and one guy said, 'Yep, we had a report of Bigfoot.' I said, come on, you're pulling my leg, and he said, 'Oh no.' This driver, who was a Mormon bishop from a little town in Utah, was driving on his daily run. He had been at the test site for many years, never drank…he was not the kind of guy to be a practical joker. He said he saw this big hairy beast go across the road in front of him."

The security officer at the site provided Jackson with another interesting tidbit:

"There were big footprints that went out across the desert and absolutely disappeared!"

Once the story was out, Jackson fielded calls from reporters and radio stations from across the country. He even spoke to a Bigfoot researcher from the Northwest.

"I described the thing to him, and he said, 'That's typical.' And I said, well, what about the footprints disappearing? And he said, 'Oh, that's typical.'"

Just when Jackson thought the calls couldn't get any odder, they did. He recalls the man on the phone who stated:

"You're not going to believe a word I tell you."

The man asked what direction the footprints were headed.

"East into the desert. He had already passed a pretty good desert to get there," Jackson told him. The man replied, telling Jackson:

"Well, whenever we have a sighting of a Bigfoot heading east, there's going to be an earthquake within twenty-four hours."

A strange claim to be sure, one that Jackson didn't quite know what to do with, but the real kicker came the next day when there was a reported 6.8 earthquake in the Owens Valley, a location in California that the reported creature may have been heading away from.

Between fascinating Native American legends and modern encounters, there's a rich and mysterious history of monsters in the wilds of Nevada. So next time you're in sin city pulling back the handle on a slot machine and waiting to hit the jackpot, just remember, out there across the deserts and in the mountains, there may be something large and hairy in the shadows.

References:

"Legends of Spirit Cave," Dennis Cassinelli

"Life Among Piutes: Their Wrongs and Claims" Sarah Winnemucca Hopkins.

NevadaSasquatch.blogspot.com

"Weird Las Vegas and Nevada: Your Alternative Travel Guide to Sin City and the Silver State." Joe Oesterle and Tim Cridland.

Contributor Biographies

Eric Altman

Eric was born in the small town of Greensburg in Southwestern Pennsylvania. Horror and Science fiction movies filled a good portion of his childhood, leading to a lifelong interest in the strange and unusual.

His early life was filled with books, magazines and all things paranormal.

In 1980, he was inspired by two films. Legend of Boggy Creek and the Creature from Black Lake. They became his catalysts to study the Bigfoot phenomena. From a broad focus on the paranormal his attention turned to Bigfoot, the Abominable Snowman, the Yowie and other man-like creatures.

In 1983, Eric met Stan Gordon at a UFO/Bigfoot event. Stan would become Eric's mentor. For the next 19 years, Eric researched and educated himself on the Bigfoot phenomena not just in his region, but nationally and globally.

After attending a Bigfoot Conference in Ohio in 1997, Eric decide to devote more time investigating sightings in his home state of Pennsylvania, forming the Southwestern Pennsylvania Bigfoot Study Group. He was also appointed as the BFRO's (Bigfoot Field Researcher's Organization) point of contact for Pennsylvania.

In May 2016, Eric founded the Pennsylvania Cryptozoology Society, a group of volunteers dedicated to investigating strange animal and cryptid cases in PA and surrounding states.

Eric has investigated over 300 cases around the country. Eric holds positions in multiple research groups and often follows up on PA Bigfoot reports for Cliff Barackman from Finding Bigfoot.

Over the years, Eric has organized and hosted eight East Coast Bigfoot Conferences. His research and work has been featured in countless media outlets including books, magazines, television and radio.

He has appeared in Mountain Devil: The Search for Frank Peterson and American Sasquatch Hunters: Bigfoot in America.

He is also the co-founder of Beyond the Edge Radio, a live show featured on the Para-X Radio Network and Planet Paranormal.

http://www.ericaltman.net/

Loren Coleman

Loren Coleman is one of the world's leading cryptozoologists. An honorary member of the British Columbia Scientific Cryptozoology Club, and several other international organizations, he is also a Life Member of the International Society of Cryptozoology. Starting his fieldwork and investigations in 1960, after traveling and trekking extensively in pursuit of cryptozoological mysteries, Coleman began writing to share his experiences in 1969.

Coleman has written seventeen books and more than three hundred articles, has appeared frequently on radio and television programs, and has lectured throughout North America, as well as in London and at Loch Ness. He has been both on- and off-camera consultant to NBC-TV's "Unsolved Mysteries," A & E's "Ancient Mysteries," History Channel's "In Search of History," Discovery Channel's "In the Unknown," and other reality-based programs. He contributes cryptozoology columns, "On the Trail," to the London-based magazine Fortean Times, and "Mysterious World" to Fate, as well as regular articles to the Anomalist and Fortean Studies. In 2000, he served as the Senior Series Consultant to the new "In Search Of…" program which is scheduled for future broadcast on Fox and USA Network. During 2002, he was featured in the Sony Studios' "Search of the Mothman," available on the DVD of the movie "The Mothman Prophecies." He served as the Screen Gems' national and international publicity spokesperson for their Richard Gere-Mark Pellington movie.

Loren has been investigating in the field and in the library, cryptozoological evidence and folklore since the Abominable Snowmen caught his interest over four decades ago, leading him to research mysterious Black Panther sightings and reports of Napes (North American Apes) in the American Midwest. He has traveled to every state in the USA, throughout Canada, Mexico, Scotland, and the Virgin Islands, interviewing witnesses of Lake Monsters, Bigfoot, Giant Snakes, Mystery Felids, Mothman, Thunderbirds, and other cryptids.

His first article was published in 1969. He went on to write two books with Jerome Clark (The Unidentified [1975] and Creatures of the Outer Edge [1978], both published by Warner Books). In the 1980s, Coleman wrote Mysterious America (1983), Curious Encounters (1985), and Tom Slick and the Search for the Yeti (1989), all bestsellers for Faber and Faber. In 1999 Loren Coleman co-authored two books: one with Patrick Huyghe called The Field Guide to Bigfoot, Yeti and Other Mystery Primates Worldwide (Avon), the other with Jerome Clark called Cryptozoology A to Z: The Encyclopedia of Loch Monsters, Sasquatch, Chupacabras, and Other Authentic Mysteries of Nautre (Simon and Schuster/Fireside). During 2002, Linden published the biography, Tom Slick: True Life Encounters in Cryptozoology.

Coleman's extremely popular Mysterious America: The Revised Edition (2001) and Mothman and Other Curious Encounters (2002) are published by Paraview Press.

Obtaining an undergraduate degree from Southern Illinois University-Carbondale, Coleman majored in anthropology, minored in zoology, and did some summer work in archaeology. He received a graduate degree in psychiatric social work from Simmons College in Boston. Coleman was admitted to the Ph.D. programs, and took doctoral coursework in social anthropology at Brandies University, and in sociology at the University of New Hampshire's Family Research Laboratory.

Coleman has been an instructor, assistant/associate professor, research associate, and documentary filmmaker, in various academic university settings, since 1980. He gave one of the first credit courses on the subject of cryptozoology in 1990, and examined cryptozoology films in his popular documentary course he taught through 2003 at the University of Southern Maine.

http://lorencoleman.com/

Richard Freeman

Richard Freeman is a cryptozoologist, author, zoological journalist, WebTV Presenter, and zoological director of the Centre for Fortean Zoology (CFZ). Freeman has written, co-written, or edited a number of books, and has contributed widely to both Fortean and zoological magazines, as well as other newspapers and periodicals, including Fortean Times and Paranormal Magazine.

He has lectured across the UK at the Fortean Times Unconvention, the Weird Weekend, Microcon, the Natural History Museum, the Grant Museum of Zoology, Queen Mary, University of London and the Last Tuesday Society. All on pursuit of the Tasmanian wolf, orang-pendek, Mongolian deathworm, yeti, giant anaconda, almasty, ninki-nanka, Scottish and English lake monsters.

Richard credits an early obsession with the classic science fictions series Doctor Who (with Jon Pertwee) as sparking an interest in all things weird. After school, he became a zoo keeper at Twycross Zoo in Leicestershire and became head keeper of reptiles, working with more than 400 exotic species from ants to elephants (but with a special interest in crocodilians). After leaving the zoo, he worked in an exotic pet shop, a reptile rescue centre, and as a gravedigger.

Whilst on holiday he learned of the CFZ and bought a copy of the Centre's journal, Animals & Men, which left him impressed enough to subscribe and begin contributing. He eventually became the CFZ's Yorkshire representative, then moved to Devon to become a full-time member of the Centre. He is now the zoological director and co-editor of Animals & Men and the annual CFZ yearbook.

Rosemary Ellen Guiley

Rosemary Ellen Guiley is a researcher and author in the paranormal, UFO, metaphysical and cryptid fields. She is the author of more than 65 books, including nine encyclopedia and reference works. She hosts Strange Dimensions, a weekly radio show on KGRA Digital Broadcasting, and runs an independent publishing and media company, Visionary Living, Inc. She is a frequent guest on Coast to Coast AM with George Noory. In addition, Rosemary serves on the boards of directors of the Edgar Mitchell Foundation for Research into Extraterrestrial Encounters and the Academy for Spiritual and Consciousness Studies. Her websites are:

http://www.visionaryliving.com/

http://djinnuniverse.com/

Christopher O'Brien

From 1992 to 2002 investigative journalist Christopher O'Brien investigated and/or logged hundreds of unexplained events reported in the San Luis Valley—located in South-Central Colorado/North Central New Mexico. Working with law enforcement officials from area counties, ex-military members, ranchers and an extensive network of skywatcher/investigators, he documented what may have been the most intense wave of unexplained activity ever seen in a single region of North America. His ten-plus year investigation resulted in the three books of his "mysterious valley" trilogy, The Mysterious Valley, Enter the Valley, (both St Martins Press) and Secrets of the Mysterious Valley. His field investigation of UFO reports, unexplained livestock deaths, Native American legends, cryptozoological animals, secret military activity and the folklore, found in the world's largest alpine valley, has produced one of the largest databases of unusual occurrences gathered from a single geographic region.

His new book Stalking the Herd (600 pages 2014) is the most comprehensive book ever written on the subject of "cattle mutilations." It is destined to become the go-to textbook examining this complicated mystery.

He is also an "experiencer" having had a close encounter w/ a bigfoot at the base of Mt. Shasta in the early spring of 1979.

O'Brien has appeared on over 70 TV show segments and documentaries and hundreds radio programs around the world including, Ancient Aliens, Coast to Coast, UFO Hunters, Inside

Edition, Extra, Sightings, Unsolved Mysteries, Unexplained Files and his investigations have been featured by the History, Learning, Travel and Discovery Channels, the BBC, Nippon TV, the Associated Press, Denver Post, Albuquerque Journal, Fate, UFO Magazine and many other publications and media outlets too numerous too mention.

He has location-scouted, field-produced, supplied footage for dozens of production companies and directed two segments for the TV show Strange Universe. He is currently an associate producer for Ronald James Films, and his film (co-produced with Ron James and Jennifer Stein) "It Could Happen Tomorrow" won two 2012 EBE film festival Awards—for Best Feature and The Peoples Choice Award.

https://www.ourstrangeplanet.com/

Sam Shearon

Sam Shearon is an English dark artist born in Liverpool, England. Specializing in horror and science-fiction, his work often includes elements inspired by vintage tales of monsters and madmen, dark futures, post-apocalyptic genres and classic literature including H.P.Lovecraft's The Call of Cthulhu, Oscar Wilde's The Picture of Dorian Gray and the modern classics Clive Barker's Hellraiser and the Books of Blood all of which he has fully illustrated.

Shearon's main influences stem from ancient cultures, the occult, industrial/art/revolution-eras, the supernatural, the paranormal, cryptozoology and the unexplained. Shearon has created covers for comic books and graphic novels including Clive Barker's HELLRAISER, The X-Files, Mars Attacks, 30 Days of Night, Angel, KISS, and more.

He has created album art and merchandise designs for some of the biggest names in rock music including Iron Maiden, Rob Zombie and Godhead.

Shearon studied at the University of Leeds in the College of Art & Design, West Yorkshire, England. He was awarded a Bachelor of Arts Degree with Honors in 2000 for Visual Communication. Shortly after, he went on to become a qualified Art teacher gaining a Post-Graduate Certificate in Education from Huddersfield University. His first solo exhibition entitled "A Walk on the Darkside" in 2003, featured forty-five pieces of his original artwork including 6-foot-tall (1.8 m) demonic statues, biomechanical monsters and giant canvases depicting images of horror and the macabre. The exhibition was featured in various national newspapers including The Daily Telegraph as well as BBC Radio One and live interviews on BBC Radio Leeds North. The show attracted protests and boycotts over its inclusion of animal bones, and the mutilation and disembowelment of children's toys, but the show was extended to six weeks due to popular demand.

His work has been described by the British press as "bizarre," "grotesque," "gruesome," and "groundbreaking." Shearon is known for his work in the field of cryptozoology, most notably for compiling artists impressions, of the Beast of Lytham from eyewitness accounts. Shearon's cryptozoological art was on display at the 2005 Weird Weekend, an annual conference at the Centre for Fortean Zoology. His work can be found in publications of the Fortean Times, Paranormal Magazine and other cryptozoology and paranormal publications.

http://www.mister-sam.com

Dave Spinks

After experiencing an after death visit from his grandfather, Dave Spinks became fascinated by the paranormal and started his search for answers. Gathering evidence in the form of EVPs, video and photographic data and personal experiences. Dave collected experiences from everyone he could and sites "In Search Of," with Leonard Nimoy as an early influence.

As an adult, he joined the USAF right out of college and became a trained observer. He spent nine years in the military, eight in the Air Force and one in the Army National Guard in a Military Police unit.

After active duty, Dave pursued a career in law enforcement and studied criminal justice in college. He became a Federal Law Enforcement officer and spent eight years working for the US Department of Justice.

His professional path greatly enhanced his investigative experience. During his years working for the Government, he continued his pursuit of the paranormal and investigated every time he had an opportunity.

His service gave him the chance to investigate international locations in Italy while stationed there in the 1990s.

In 2011, he retired from Law Enforcement and decided to pursue paranormal investigation on a full-time basis.

"I like to share what I do with others, in the hopes of answering some of man's greatest questions: Is there life after death? Are there unknown creatures walking among us? Are we alone in the universe? I believe we are not alone, and finding answers is my motivation."

http://www.davespinksparanormalinvestigator.com/

Jeff Stewart

Jeff Stewart was born in Carthage, Texas and raised in the woods and wetlands along the Sabine river. Jeff attended Tenaha high school then Baptist Christian University. After leaving Baptist Christian, Jeff attended the University of Colorado School of Mines where he received a degree in Mining Electronics. Jeff holds degrees in Theology and a certificate as a Veterinary Technician and Animal Rescuer Wildlife Rehabilitator. Jeff is also an ordained Minister.

Jeff is a columnist and blogger for Texas Fish and Game Magazine and one of the most respected wildlife experts in the state of Texas.

Jeff grew up hunting and fishing the woods of East Texas and was taught to hunt, fish, trap and track by "some of the best there ever was." (at least in his eyes).

Jeff has been a Cryptozoologist and Cryptid researcher for over 20 years. Working primarily in the East Texas Pine forests and hardwood swamps along the Sabine river. Jeff has appeared on Monsters and Mysteries in America, Survivorman Bigfoot and Finding Bigfoot. Jeff also worked as a Content Creator for Destination America.

Jeff is currently the Executive Vice President of the International Cryptozoological Research Alliance.

Jeff has had his amazing encounters and research covered in several books and television shows including the Wood Knocks series.

Arbra Dale Triplett

Arbra Dale Triplett is an author, journalist, copywriter, veteran and editor. He's been writing fiction, advertising, marketing and UFO-related content for more than twenty years. Born in Springfield, Missouri to an Air Force family, he grew up in Texas, Colorado and Illinois before spending thirteen years in Germany. He studied English and History at Oklahoma Christian University, Harding University and Lubbock Christian. He served abroad in the Marine Corps for 4 years, drove semi trucks from coast to coast hauling anything from live bees to oversized freight, and flew in the Air Force as a Loadmaster on a C-130 cargo transport. He's hung his hat from Alaska to Florida and a lot of places in between. He has had a life long fascination with the unexplained, and has a soft spot for those who seek the truth. He is the author of Halcyon's Wake: Faith, and Benjamin Oliver Flanagan. His edited works include Paternus, by Dark Ashton; Strange Intruders, Men In Black, Haunted Toys, Wood Knocks, My Haunted Journal, by David Weatherly and Ross Allison; and Hunting Apes in America by Jerry Hestand. He makes his home on Table Rock Lake in the Missouri Ozarks. Need an editor for your own works? Then reach out to Dale on Twitter @DaleTriplett or on Facebook.

David Weatherly

David Weatherly is a renaissance man of the strange and supernatural. He has traveled the world in pursuit of ghosts, cryptids, UFOs, magic, and more. From the specters of dusty castles, to remote, haunted islands, from ancient sites, to modern mysteries, he has journeyed to the most unusual places on the globe seeking the unknown.

David became fascinated with the paranormal at a young age. Ghost stories and accounts of weird creatures and UFOs led him to discover many of his early influences. Writers such as such as John Keel, Jacques Vallee, Hans Holzer and others set him on course to spend his life exploring and investigating the unexplained.

Throughout his life, he's also delved into shamanic and magical traditions from around the world, spending time with elders from numerous cultures in Europe, the Americas, Africa and Asia. He has studied with Taoist masters in China, Tibetan Lamas, and other mystics from the far east. He's picked up knowledge from African and Native American tribal elders and sat around fires with shaman from countless other traditions.

Along his path, David has also gathered a lot of arcane knowledge, studying a range of ancient arts from palmistry, the runes, and other obscure forms of divination, to alchemy and magick. He has studied and taught Qigong and Ninjutsu, as well as various energy related arts. David has also studied stage and performance magic.

His shamanic and magical background has given him a unique

perspective in his explorations into the unknown, and he continues to write, travel and explore, leaving no stone unturned in his quest for the strange and unusual.

David has investigated, and written about, a diverse range of topics including, Hauntings & Ghosts, Cryptozoology, Ufology, Ancient Mysteries, Shamanism, Magic and Psychic Phenomena.

In 2012, David founded an independent media and publishing company.

He has been a featured speaker at conferences around the world and has lectured for countless paranormal and spiritual groups.

He is a frequent guest on Coast to Coast AM with George Noory, Spaced Out Radio and other radio programs. David has also appeared on numerous television shows including the Travel Channel's Mysteries of the Outdoors, History Channel's Ancient Aliens, Beyond Belief and other programs.

David has written numerous books including Strange Intruders, Black Eyed Children and the "Haunted" series.

Find David online at:

https://eerielights.com/

Made in the USA
Columbia, SC
20 December 2021